WISCONSIN TALK

Languages and Folklore of the Upper Midwest

JOSEPH SALMONS *and* JAMES P. LEARY, *Series Editors*

Published in collaboration with the Center for the Study of Upper Midwestern Cultures at the University of Wisconsin–Madison

The Tamburitza Tradition: From the Balkans to the American Midwest

RICHARD MARCH

Wisconsin Talk: Linguistic Diversity in the Badger State

Edited by THOMAS PURNELL, ERIC RAIMY, *and* JOSEPH SALMONS

WISCONSIN TALK

Linguistic Diversity in the Badger State

Edited by THOMAS PURNELL, ERIC RAIMY,
and JOSEPH SALMONS

THE UNIVERSITY OF WISCONSIN PRESS

The University of Wisconsin Press
1930 Monroe Street, 3rd Floor
Madison, Wisconsin 53711-2059
uwpress.wisc.edu

3 Henrietta Street
London WC2E 8LU, England
eurospanbookstore.com

Library of Congress Cataloging-in-Publication Data

Wisconsin talk : linguistic diversity in the Badger State / edited by Thomas Purnell,
Eric Raimy, and Joseph Salmons.
p. cm. — (Languages and folklore of the Upper Midwest)
Includes bibliographical references and index.
ISBN 978-0-299-29334-5 (pbk. : alk. paper) — ISBN 978-0-299-29333-8 (e-book)
1. Wisconsin—Languages. 2. English language—Wisconsin.
3. English language—Dialects—Wisconsin. I. Purnell, Thomas C. II. Raimy, Eric.
III. Salmons, Joe, 1956– IV. Series: Languages and folklore of the Upper Midwest.
PE3101.W5W57 2013
409.775—dc23
2012037480

Contents

Foreword

PEYTON SMITH

When I was asked to write a foreword for this book, my first thought was "Yah hey, I'll do this once, now." That initial, internal response no doubt came from the years I spent growing up in Sheboygan, Wisconsin, coupled with my intense pride as a lifelong Wisconsin resident. In all seriousness, I was thrilled to be part of this fantastic work, which explores our accents and explains why the way we say things really matters to us. While Wisconsinites may all sound the same to some, as my brother-in-law from California often points out, our distinct community dialects and accents are truly rich and varied, and they make up a strong aspect of who we are.

Wisconsin citizens, scholars, and students of language throughout the country and around the world will find this book to be a great treasure. We should be thankful for the energy and talents of three editors who saw this project through, from inception to publication: Joseph Salmons, Thomas Purnell, and Eric Raimy of the University of Wisconsin–Madison. Salmons, who is a professor of German and a director of the Center for the Study of Upper Midwestern Cultures, provides insight into dialect, language, and immigration; Purnell, an associate professor of English, applies knowledge of sounds, dialect, and ethnicity; and Raimy, also an associate professor of English, brings understanding of sounds, language change, and acquisition to the work. Eight other contributors bring additional expertise in English, and other languages (native, new, and old), history, social networks, community structure, immigration, and mapping.

This book captures two long-standing traditions at UW–Madison: the Wisconsin Idea, a core value that encourages faculty and staff to reach out to the people of the state and beyond, sharing and applying practical and relevant knowledge and expertise; and the publication of seminal works about Wisconsin—its geography, fish, birds, mammals, vegetation, and Indian mounds—by the University of Wisconsin Press. This book will serve as a long-lasting, valuable resource on the scholarship of language.

Now, full disclosure: I saw the genesis of this book in fall 2008, when the authors first requested funding to work with four Wisconsin communities to better understand how language matters to the people of the state. Frankly, as chair of the UW–Madison Ira and Ineva Reilly Baldwin Wisconsin Idea Endowment committee, I was dubious. I typically read as many as 150 top-notch proposals each year from faculty, staff, and students for projects that would form partnerships with community organizations to solve problems or enhance opportunities. Yet the endowment can only fund eight to twelve projects annually. I knew it would be tough for this proposal to compete with a wealth of ideas about improving K-12 education, increasing access to health care, bolstering economic development, and more.

But after reading the proposal, which was developed following community presentations and discussions on language and which proposed bringing together a dozen scholars on Wisconsin's languages, I quickly changed my mind. The project would explore fascinating misconceptions, such as that today's immigrants don't learn English as quickly as their grandparents did, that black Americans talk very differently from white Americans, and that native and immigrant language and dialect differences are dying out.

Each belief reveals a problematic interpretation of language, identity, and society. For instance, the belief that earlier immigrants quickly learned English, while current immigrants refuse to do so, is false: "Wisconsin Germans often didn't learn English into the third generation; today's immigrants learn it as fast as they can," the editors wrote in their proposal. The issue of how immigrants acquire and use language today has been extremely divisive in many parts of the country, and it continues to influence social, education, economic, and legal policies. Furthermore, research shows that African Americans, contrary to beliefs that they are "lazy" when it comes to English, carefully balance adapting their use of the language to that of white speakers while also retaining cultural distinctiveness. And lastly, language dialects are increasing today—not declining—and many of our native languages are experiencing resurgence.

Our committee chose to fund the proposal, and the editors and others began working closely with public libraries, historical societies, teachers, heritage groups, and more in four areas of Wisconsin: Milwaukee, Rhinelander, Mineral Point, and Wausau. Overall, the project noted specific local language issues and concerns, mapped details about the community and its languages, provided knowledge and tools for further linguistic exploration, held public forums in each community, and helped to inform this book.

The project uncovered interesting facts about past and present languages in Wisconsin. Our state is home to English, German, Native American (including Ho-Chunk, Menominee, and Ojibwe), Scandinavian (including Danish, Finnish, Norwegian, and Swedish), Spanish, and Hmong, along with a smattering of many other languages of the world. While the use of Spanish and Hmong are increasing throughout the state, the project revealed that older languages still have a strong hold. For example, in Manitowoc, 1 percent of the nearly 32,000 people still spoke German at home in 2000; and in Wausau, 14 percent of the 36,000 people spoke languages other than English at home, including 3,200 Hmong and 378 German speakers. While residents of the eastern parts of Wisconsin are immersed in German language heritage, for people living in the northern counties bordering Minnesota, it is the Scandinavian languages—Norwegian, in particular—that are part of their cultural heritage and context.

This information is important not only for the people of Wisconsin; it also has international relevance. One Reilly Baldwin Wisconsin Idea Endowment committee member, Jane Pearlmutter, who at the time was associate director of the School of Library and Information Studies at UW–Madison, found that the information she used from the project was instrumental in attaining a Goethe Institute grant to extend the university's partnerships with German library schools and libraries:

> [Another factor that addresses why UW would be a strong partner for prospective exchanges] is Wisconsin's German immigrant population, whose influence is still felt throughout the state. Even today, a century after the peak of immigration, half of Wisconsin's population claims some German heritage. . . . While German librarians may be aware that American public libraries often offer Spanish-language materials, they are generally surprised to learn that at one time there were many German-speaking communities in America, with numerous German-language newspapers, and it was quite possible for at least the first generation of German immigrants in Wisconsin to manage without English language literacy.

Clearly, language really does matter to countries, to states, to local communities, and to individuals. On a personal level, although I had to lose my "Sheboyganese" dialect and accent many years ago when I had a regional radio show, to this day I get a warm, fuzzy feeling inside whenever I hear the language that surrounded me as I grew up. I love hearing phrases such as *going down by* rather than *going to*, or *come here once* rather than simply *come here*, or the distinctive, sing-song *oooouu-uuhhhhhhhh* vowel sounds when someone pronounces *house, about, roof, coat, boat,* or *show*. Hearing the language of my youth gives me the same pleasure as eating comfort food or smelling my grandmother's house—the dialects and accents bring back good memories and a sense of well-being and belonging. And, I have to say, my heart melts when my wife, a transplant to Wisconsin, says, "Yah but" in a Sheboygan accent.

Whether you have links to Wisconsin's older languages or newer languages, this book demonstrates that our state continues to advance dialects and accents that are unique to our culture. We are fortunate to have scholars who happily spent time with the folks of Wisconsin to produce this gem. Thank you, editors and authors. Thank you, readers, for picking up this book. And thank you, UW Press, for continuing to publish books that delve into what makes Wisconsin and its people unique.

Yah hey, I think I'll go read this once now, hey!

Preface

Why Language Matters for Wisconsin

JOSEPH SALMONS

If you're reading this book, you probably have some connection to the state of Wisconsin. In fact, you may live here or have lived here. If so, think about your own family and others who lived here just a couple of generations back. Vast numbers of Wisconsinites in, say, 1900, lived their lives in other languages—Ho-Chunk or Ojibwe, Polish or German—and may or may not have known English at all, and many more had limited knowledge of English and preferred their own native tongues. Even those who did speak English as a first language spoke it differently from the way it is spoken in the state today. The famous (if problematic) "Hill map" (see fig. P.1) gives one snapshot of the immigrant landscape for 1940, and that "ethnic pattern" corresponds broadly to linguistic patterns: Dutch and Czech, Finnish, and Icelandic were spoken in roughly the places indicated. (Among the problems with the map is that it doesn't give the distribution of Wisconsin's Native American communities at the time; see chapter 2.)

Today, most of those older immigrant languages are less widely spoken, while Native languages are the focus of intense revitalization efforts. At the same time, new languages have come into the state in large numbers, like Hmong and Spanish. Everyone is aware of those communities, but many are less familiar with the influx of speakers of indigenous Central American languages like Mixtec and Yucatec, who learned Spanish as a second or third language. A far more visible

FIGURE P.1. A popular presentation of the "Hill map," showing the "national roots" of the people of Wisconsin, created by University of Wisconsin–Madison sociologist George W. Hill in 1941 (Courtesy of the Wisconsin Historical Society, image ID WHi-62099)

recently arrived, if not well understood, language is Pennsylvania Dutch, also known as Pennsylvania German. It's spoken by a rapidly growing population of Old Order Amish (and Old Order Mennonites) in the state, probably around ten thousand at this writing. In-migration of Amish and Mennonites from other parts of the United States is one reason why the number of people speaking the language in Wisconsin is growing, but another reason is that these communities have large families. Pennsylvania Dutch is a distinctly American language, forged from a set of German dialects in the eighteenth century and following its own path of development since. It's unlike most other minority languages in North America in that the number of speakers is growing: in Old Order Amish and Mennonite communities, it's still being learned and used by children. As we'll see throughout the book, most other languages in Wisconsin—and to an alarming extent, around the world—are losing speakers and most are predicted to die out in the coming century or so.

The next four maps (figs. P.2, P.3, P.4, and P.5) should give you a first impression of the changes that have occurred since the Hill map, an impression to be sharpened and refined in maps through the coming chapters, as well as by additional maps on our website (http://csumc .wisc.edu/wep). The first simply shows the percentage of people who reported in 2000 to the census that they spoke some language other than English at home, while the second gives the most recent information available, from the American Community Survey, by county.

Now let's zoom in to one area of the state—the southeastern corner— and look not just at the size of the non-English-speaking population but also at the distribution of which languages are represented within that population. You can see that Spanish speakers are heavily represented in these mostly urban counties (see chapter 9). Other Indo-European languages include the traditional immigrant languages of Wisconsin (German, Polish) and some newer ones (Russian, for example), and these make up a considerable part of the total, especially in suburban Waukesha County. The Asian and Pacific Islander group includes the Hmong (see chapter 8). While they are often associated with western and central Wisconsin, you see here that many have moved to the southeast.

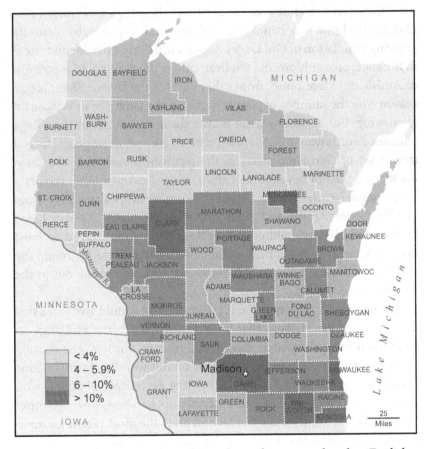

FIGURE P.2. Percentage of people speaking a language other than English at home, 2006–10, by county (Data from the American Community Survey 2006–10, five-year estimates, table DP02, "Selected Social Characteristics in the United States")

At the same time, English itself has been transformed here: in the last decades, almost all the features that people now associate with a "Wisconsin accent" have come into existence, or at least established themselves. And all of them are changing today, spreading or receding, generalizing or becoming more restricted in some way.

In short, Wisconsin is extremely rich linguistically, it has been since long before the name Wisconsin existed, and it's getting richer today. But what about that name? *Wisconsin* is readily recognizable to folks in

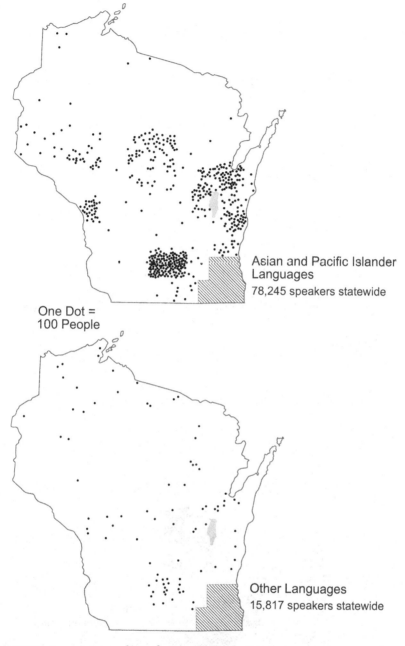

One Dot =
100 People

Asian and Pacific Islander
Languages
78,245 speakers statewide

Other Languages
15,817 speakers statewide

FIGURE P.3. Asian and Pacific Islander and other languages, 2006–10, by county. Asian languages include Hmong, Japanese, and Thai; "other" languages include Native American languages and Finnish. (Data from the American Community Survey 2006–10, five-year estimates, table DP02, "Selected Social Characteristics in the United States")

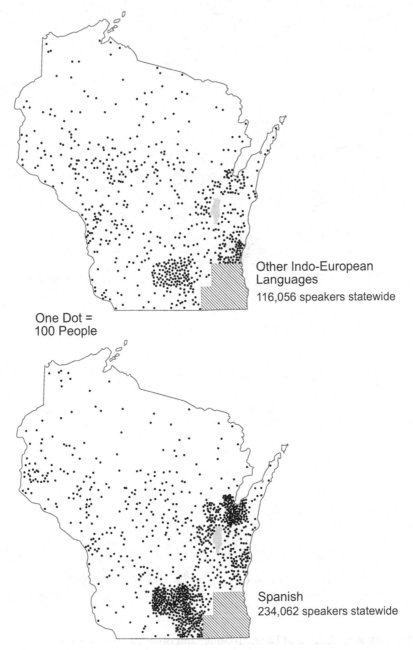

Other Indo-European
Languages
116,056 speakers statewide

One Dot =
100 People

Spanish
234,062 speakers statewide

FIGURE P.4. Other Indo-European languages and Spanish, 2006–10, by county. Other Indo-European languages include German and Norwegian. (Data from the American Community Survey 2006–10, five-year estimates, table DP02, "Selected Social Characteristics in the United States")

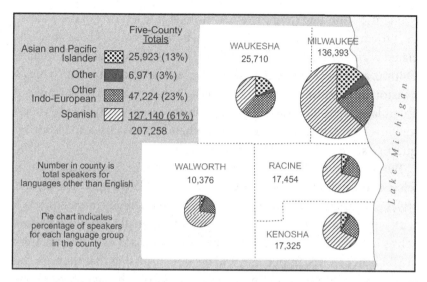

FIGURE P.5. Percentage of people speaking a language other than English at home, southeast Wisconsin, 2006–10 (Data from the American Community Survey, 2006–10, five-year estimates, table DP02, "Selected Social Characteristics in the United States")

the Upper Midwest as a name of Native origin, like many distinctive place names in the region. (Just think of the "you must be from Wisconsin if . . ." lines that include answers like "you know how to pronounce Oconomowoc.") The story of Wisconsin as a name shows how uncertain and complex language history can be. According to the best sources (Cassidy 1991 and Vogel 1991; for a summary, see http://www.wisconsinhistory.org/topics/wisconsin-name), the original name is first recorded in writing by Father Marquette in 1673 as the river name Meskousing, based on what he heard from Miami guides who took him to the river en route to the Mississippi. Spelling, to the surprise of many nonlinguists, is one of the least important and interesting aspects of language and language change, but here it plays a crucial role: the initial *M* was later miscopied in many variants as *Ou* (a spelling for the *w* sound in French, like in *oui*), which stuck, and eventually got anglicized as *Wiskonsan* or *Wisconsin*. Beyond that, the trail goes cold. There are lots of wild and not-so-wild proposals for meanings from the

Romantic-sounding (and extremely unlikely) "gathering of the waters" to "little muskrat house" and "toward where it is cold." These are associated with (among other languages) Ho-Chunk, Menominee, Miami, Ojibwe, and French. But none of them are close to compelling to me as a historical linguist. You can take this as a cautionary tale for thinking about language: sometimes, history has obscured the tracks too much to allow firm conclusions, and even when it comes to contemporary questions, we often know less than we think.

But let's return to the broader topic. Language is a central part of what makes us human, and how we speak—what languages, dialects, and styles of speaking we learn and use—are fundamentally interconnected with who we are—personally, socially, and regionally—how we fit ourselves into the world around us, and how others see us. These matters are, in other words, important, and it's not surprising that they are the topic of regular discussion in our daily lives, from the languages of our ancestors (whether they've lived here for thousands of years or a few years) to distinct features of our English, but reliable information is all too often lacking. This book grows from an effort to begin filling that gap.

The three coeditors of this volume came as adults to Wisconsin, where we now work and live, from other parts of the country: Tom Purnell is from Ithaca, New York (and other places), Eric Raimy hails from Erie, Pennsylvania, and I grew up in Kings Mountain, North Carolina. We'd all lived in various other parts of the United States, and when we arrived, we all realized how linguistically rich Wisconsin is and how rich it has been for centuries. About a decade ago, Tom and I began working on issues in the pronunciation of English here, and I was already working on German as an immigrant language in the state. And we were also in close contact with colleagues working on Native languages and other immigrant languages. From this, the Wisconsin Englishes Project was born, and Eric joined the group as soon as he arrived. Our project website (http://csumc.wisc.edu/wep) gives information on that large and continuing effort, and the site is being supplemented, updated, and expanded in connection with the publication of this volume.

While there hasn't been very much contemporary research on some aspects of language and dialect in Wisconsin, we were able to start our research and outreach efforts from a relatively advanced stage of understanding and have been able to produce a volume like this thanks to a remarkable tradition of research on language and dialect in the state. Take a couple of examples: Leonard Bloomfield (1887–1949) grew up in part in Elkhart Lake, Wisconsin, and did some of his graduate work in Madison. While he spent his career elsewhere, he came back to do fieldwork on the Menominee language, and he wrote a massive grammar of it, along with a large dictionary and a set of texts in it. Einar Haugen (1906–94) was from Iowa but taught at UW–Madison for over thirty years. He was a Norwegian-English bilingual, and his tome *The Norwegian Language in America* (1953) remains one of the most important works on immigrant languages in the United States even today. Frederic Cassidy (1907–2000) was from Jamaica but spent decades studying English in Wisconsin, most famously as the founder and leader of the *Dictionary of American Regional English*. (The last volume was published by Harvard University Press in 2012.) Lester W. J. "Smoky" Seifert (1915–96) was from Juneau, Wisconsin, raised with his family's Oderbrüchisch dialect, alongside (Standard) German and English. His dissertation was a seminal study of Pennsylvania German, but he returned to teach at UW–Madison for decades, where his work was key to the mission of the Max Kade Institute on campus. He made recordings of German and German dialects in the 1940s that provide us with critical insight into how that language developed in Wisconsin over time. (Those recordings are housed at the Max Kade Institute on campus.)

The connection to these people for us is realer and more direct than most people imagine: The authors of chapter 1 still use Bloomfield's grammar of Menominee to understand that language today. Our work on German in the state is shaped by Smoky Seifert's recordings; nowhere else in the German-speaking diaspora is there such a rich and early trove of materials, especially for what we might call "American Standard German." The same holds for Haugen's work on Norwegian in the Upper Midwest. And Cassidy's fieldwork provides us with a set of audio recordings from around the state from the early 1950s and also from across the United States in the late 1960s. We use their recordings and build on their analyses constantly, and we are able to understand the present far better thanks to their interpretations of an earlier period. We really stand on the shoulders of giants.

In this little book, we've included chapters that should show you something about the range of languages and dialects spoken here—Native American languages, older and newer immigrant languages, and kinds of English—and about issues of language variation and education. But each of these matters also makes a bigger point (or several) about language. Chapter 1 describes not only the diversity of Wisconsin's Indian languages but also tells a story of linguistic resilience after a history of efforts to force communities to adopt English, a local example of the worldwide problem of language endangerment. Chapters 2 and 3 explore issues of classic nineteenth-century waves of immigration to Wisconsin with which the state is closely associated. The first outlines community formation and institutional support for languages, and the second provides a case study of one language, German, in schools, showing important parallels to the situation for new immigrants today. Chapter 4 reveals the complexity of perceiving the immigrant past, exploring why southwestern Wisconsin is so distinct from the rest of the state in its speech patterns. Along the way, the chapter investigates the association of Mineral Point with Cornish immigrants that persists after the obvious influences on English there have faded or disappeared. One of the ways that people inevitably think of regional English is in terms of the distinct words a region has, the topic of chapter 5. Chapter 6 tackles the broadest issue about variation in English generally: what "Standard English" is and how we judge people who don't speak like us. Building on that, chapter 7 deals with the variety of English that has been most aggressively stigmatized, African American English (AAE), what some people call "Ebonics," and shows how and why it is just as much a grammatical system as any other language or dialect of a language. Just as importantly, it lays out how we perceive AAE and what that does and doesn't mean. Chapter 8 turns to newer immigrant languages, giving an overview of the situation of the Hmong in Wisconsin and showing how speakers negotiate cultural and linguistic challenges in this country. Chapter 9 addresses the growing community of Spanish speakers in Wisconsin, making clear that there isn't one homogenous "Hispanic" community and, moreover, how bilingualism is a valuable resource for us as a society. Chapter 10 tells a story that we as the editors of this volume are still grasping, namely how maps really do help convey key narratives.

Of course, there's also a lot that this book does not include, partly because we wanted to keep the book short and partly because there just isn't current research on certain topics. But maybe that just means another book will be needed down the line. There are only a few models for this kind of state linguistic profile, like Brian Joseph, Carol Preston, and Dennis Preston's *Language Diversity in Michigan and Ohio* (2005), a more in-depth survey from another part of the Midwest. At the same time, the printed book is only one small part of this project. The Wisconsin Englishes Project website, already noted a couple of times, should continue to grow. There, too, we draw inspiration from a few other projects, especially the North Carolina Language and Life Project (http://www.ncsu.edu/linguistics/ncllp) and the more recent work by a group in the Pacific Northwest, led by Kristin Denham, with a group of linguists and teachers.

Finally, while we stand on the shoulders of the giants who came before, a lot of colleagues in the present have made this work possible. Most important was the help from Mark Livengood, who, in addition to contributing a chapter, created the maps and took most of the photos for the book. We knew from the beginning that we needed a lot of maps, and Mark has worked long and hard with us to develop the maps that appear in this book and others that are on our website. We're extremely grateful for those efforts. We have also benefited tremendously from the advice and help of Joan Hall, Rob Howell, Jim Leary, Mark Louden, Ruth Olson, Antje Petty, Rand Valentine, Luanne von Schneidemesser, and many others. The University of Wisconsin Press selected two of the best peer reviewers in the field, both of whom provided extremely valuable, detailed, and constructive input that reshaped a number of chapters. Both also revealed their identities to us later, so that we can thank them by name: Michael Paul Adams and Erica Benson. UW Press staff have guided us through the process more smoothly than we could have imagined, Matt Boutilier has helped us immensely with formatting references and other tasks along the way, and Alyson Sewell has helped with the indexing. And generation after generation of students are showing us new directions that work will go in (and we're counting on them to undertake the next books on this topic!). Most immediately, this book grows from the project "Language Matters for Wisconsin: A Community-Based Initiative," generously funded by the Ira and Ineva Reilly Baldwin Wisconsin Idea Endowment (see Peyton Smith's foreword for details). But our work got started thanks to generous support from the Wisconsin Humanities Council (both a mini-grant and a major grant), and we've had critical help from the Brittingham Fund and generous funding from the UW–Madison Graduate School. As we reach the centennial of the Wisconsin Idea, we take that kind of support as evidence that it remains alive and well, even as our great university is being decimated by budget cuts.

So, enjoy the book, think about how language matters to you, and get in touch with us with stories, comments, and questions.

WISCONSIN TALK

Introduction

Thinking about Language and Wisconsin English

THOMAS PURNELL, ERIC RAIMY,
AND JOSEPH SALMONS

The chapters that follow treat a range of important issues about English, as well as about various other languages, in the state, including regional vocabulary and African American speech patterns. This chapter uses some regional English examples to introduce you to some basic issues and some of the ways that linguists think about language and kinds of language. Along the way, we take the opportunity to illustrate some salient features of English in the region. First, though, we provide a quick introduction to how we think about dialects and then to some patterns of sounds, word forms, and larger pieces of language (often called "grammar").

LABELING OUR SPEECH

When describing some salient part of a person's speech, we often use terms like *dialect, accent, brogue, lilt,* or *slang.* As linguists we use each of these with a specific meaning. Perhaps the single most important difference is between dialect—systematic variation in sounds, words and phrases associated with some regional, ethnic, or social group—and accent, referring narrowly to pronunciation. Accent is, in other words, part of dialect. One reason for splitting out accent is that very often speakers will use standard words, phrases, and the like but use an accent that is distinct. For example, a southerner teaching at a university might "sound" southern in her accent, pronouncing *I* like *aaah*, while teaching nuclear physics, using entirely standard phrases and words with all the standard meanings in nuclear physics and doing it with utterly nonregional grammar. The terms *brogue* and *lilt* also have to do with accent. *Brogue* is usually understood as a strong regional accent that is tied to location and often in particular a location affiliated with Irish heritage (e.g., parts of Boston). *Lilt* has the general meaning of the song, tune, or cadence of someone's speech. Technically, this word is often synonymous with the concept linguists call "prosody," that is, the family of features including a speaker's pitch, the duration of sounds in their speech, how they stress vowels or don't, and the relative loudness of different syllables.

We also have terms for describing variation in words. For words that sound old, there isn't a pithy word; often, then, we might say that such-and-such a word is archaic or just "old." However, for contemporary words people often use the word *slang*. Slang encompasses words or turns of phrase that are limited by domain, like youth speech. (Slang was just the topic of a wonderfully readable and informative book; see Adams 2009.) Words are easily learned and easily discarded and slang is highly variable; just think about how well you can guess someone's age by what terms they use for something that people our age might call "cool": *nifty, neato, bad, sick,* and so on. In some related contexts, *jargon* would be the preferred term. We wouldn't, say, talk about the slang of banking, but rather refer to the jargon of that profession.

With sounds (accent) and words (slang) covered, let's turn to larger chunks of language, or syntax. The lay term for syntax is *grammar*, but, once again, specialists use the term *grammar* to refer to any part of language that looks systematic. Thus, sounds and word formation processes are governed by grammar, in the technical sense. English speakers start words with the sounds *t* and *r* but not *t* and *l*, so that *tree* and *true* are words but *tlee* and *tlue* could not be. We can make similar generalizations about what prefixes or suffixes we can and can't add and about how we shorten or "clip" words. So, *syntax*—not an uncommon word itself—is preferred among linguists because it refers to how words are meaningfully placed into positions in phrases or sentences. Nonlinguists often think of grammar especially in terms of "bad" or "incorrect" grammar. While many of us were chastised in school for using "double negatives" ("I can't get no satisfaction") or constructions like "Mary and me went to school," these are old and widespread features of spoken English. Many other features fly below the "correctness" radar, like whether you say that a broken window "needs to be fixed," "needs fixing," or "needs fixed."

LANGUAGE AND GEOGRAPHY

Think back to the concept of brogue as accent tied to a particular location. Perhaps some of us lacking the Irish associations with the word could talk about the Cornish brogue (once) spoken in southwestern Wisconsin, around Mineral Point. Having this kind of term that by definition links language with geography is useful because one of the primary ways of dividing up speakers of the same language is by geography. This division has a very long history, serving as a simple and salient way of separating those inside a group from outsiders. Geographic dialectology has a rich history in the United States, and a number of regional dialect atlases catalogue words, as does the national *Dictionary of American Regional English* (Cassidy and Hall 1985–2012), housed at the University of Wisconsin–Madison.

One thing we learn from these atlases is that topographic boundaries and dialect edges don't follow state lines. For example, Wisconsinites share many features with eastern Minnesotans and northern Illinoisans. At one time, the Mississippi River may have effectively separated speakers on the western banks who pronounced the words *caught* and *cot*, which differ only by their vowel, the same way from the speakers on the eastern banks who said the words differently. Now, better transportation systems (bridges, roads, along with public transportation) allow us to cover distance so easily that the Minneapolis–St. Paul metropolitan area includes western Wisconsin, and the river's boundary properties are minimized. As we study Wisconsin more thoroughly, we'll see that some natural boundaries never really were boundaries. For example, the lead region and cheese domains identify Highway 18 in the southwest as a cultural boundary instead of the nearby Wisconsin River (see fig. I.1). We have much to learn about the

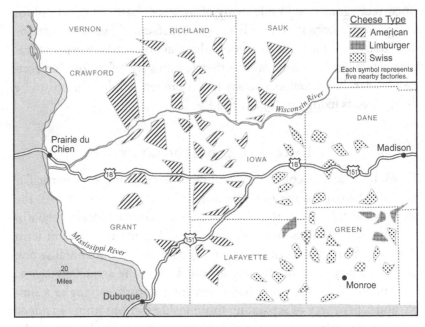

FIGURE I.1. US Highway 18 and major cheese areas in southwest
Wisconsin (Data from Conzen 1997 was generalized by connecting five
adjacent, similar data points. Each symbol, therefore, represents five directly
proximate cheese factories.)

relationship between topographical features and speech, especially as
technology and our travel patterns change the role once played by old
boundaries.

Another reason geographic boundaries can be problematic is that as
urbanization and migration continue, old coextensive boundaries (e.g.,
Welsh or Cornish in the southwest, Germans in the east, Scandina-
vians in the north and west) are broken down, so that accents, words,
and phrases originally thought of as being from one part or another of
the state can show up in another part. The loss of the vowel difference
in *caught* and *cot* and the use of *anymore* at the beginning of a phrase or
sentence ("Anymore gas is expensive") are contemporary examples of
how geographic distribution seems to be changing before our eyes.
This makes language a moving target to a much greater extent than has
traditionally been realized—many people, including linguists, had once

thought of regional differences as mostly disappearing, or dying out, but both of these usages and many more are in fact spreading today.

With that basic background, let's turn now to some major features of Wisconsin speech.

SOUNDS

Speech scientists make a gross division among the sounds of any language between vowels (sounds characterized with a lot of oral resonance, so sounds like *aaaah* that you can carry a tune with) and consonants (those with little resonance—you can't sing a melody easily with *p, t, k,* or even *s* or *z*). Let's consider the following nonsense sentence: "Sadly, I don't know—if you taught the begging tot how to etch on the edge of the bags, then maybe he'd not fight." How you say many of the words will indicate where you might be from. For example, if you say *sadly* with a diphthong (a vowel sound with two parts) as *say-uhd-ly* then, you may be from the southeastern portion of the state or areas eastward. Or if you say *know* with a monophthong (a vowel sound with only one part), then you might be from the area around the Twin Cities, where it has been reported that the *o* sound is pronounced differently than it is in the rest of the state. In Milwaukee, the vowels are typically diphthongal (as they are in Standard American English), but with a word like *know*, something else is going on, such as that speakers are producing the first part of the vowel relatively far forward in the mouth without raising really high to a *u* position.

Taught and *tot* may sound the same to you. The famous sociolinguist William Labov has said that this is the most widespread change in contemporary American English. It is fast moving and has been reported as happening within a speaker's adult lifetime (making it an odd change; most changes take place over/across generations). The collapse of these vowels means one less vowel in the English of such speakers. This collapse, or merger, reportedly began in western Pennsylvania and moved west to the coast and is now looping back on itself in the northern United States. This means that speakers around Minneapolis–St. Paul and in the southwest corner of the state are more likely than those speakers in the central part of the state to start pronouncing these two words the same (the merger will first occur in the southwest and then in the northwest).

To many speakers in the southeastern and eastern parts of the state, particularly in old German, Polish, and Dutch areas, *etch* and *edge* may sound the same (like *etch*), or almost the same. Such a pattern might seem odd to some speakers, but this collapse is a change that has its roots in these immigrant languages, which lack a distinction between "voiced" (*b, d, g,* etc.) and "voiceless" (*p, t, k,* etc.) sounds at the ends of words (e.g., German *bat* 'he/she offered' and *Bad* 'bath' sound alike, both pronounced with a final *t* sound).

For many Wisconsinites, *fight* sounds like *fuh-eet*. This change to the first part of the vowel is affectionately known as "Canadian raising" because many Canadians produce the first part of the vowel higher in the mouth. While speakers from Wisconsin don't generally sound Canadian, it is not uncommon for Wisconsinites traveling outside the state to be mistaken as Canadian. This is due in part to this kind of vowel.

Perhaps the single most important marker of a speaker from the core Upper Midwest (eastern Minnesota and Wisconsin) is to hear *bags* as rhyming with *begs*. When outsiders hear Wisconsinites pronounce words like *bag, flag,* or *rag,* they can go into hysterics. Honestly, there's nothing wrong with the vowel. It is just that its pronunciation has shifted high enough in the mouth that outsiders really notice it. This is hardly an odd change; Old English had a similar one a thousand years ago. Moreover, although it is present in the Upper Midwest as a marker, it is also present in the lower portion of Canada and the upper portion of the United States from the Midwest to western Washington State.

We've been looking here at particular individual patterns, but sometimes whole sets of sound change in interlocking, chain-like ways. If a Wisconsinite pronounces *six* like most people would say *sex, sex* like *Sauks, Sauks* like *socks, socks* like *sacks,* and *sacks* like *sakes,* then they're probably from Kenosha or areas to the south and east. This rotation of the vowels is, at a certain level of abstraction, like the famous great vowel shift from the late Middle English period (which, however, left the spelling as it was so that children hundreds of years later would have something to master in detention after school). It occurs in cities around the southern edge of the Great Lakes, from Upstate New York to just past Kenosha. Why Kenosha? We suspect that it's connected with the way that Kenosha is oriented in many ways to Chicago. For example, the commuter train stops in Kenosha and doesn't continue further into Wisconsin. Hence, people looking for work will go south rather than north and consequently interact with speakers from Illinois rather than from the rest of Wisconsin. The effects of this shift in Milwaukee, Madison, and now further north are often limited to the vowel in the word *sadly* (representing only the part of the *sacks* to *sakes* link). Oddly enough, St. Louis, Missouri, also displays this more limited effect, presumably because its nearest large neighbor of cultural relation is Chicago.

This is really just the tip of the iceberg on accent (in the sense we have defined the word) in Wisconsin. Just listening to how different words sound here in Wisconsin shows how much history one can hear when a Wisconsinite opens their mouth. A last thing we should say about the Wisconsin accent is that it is new in the grand scheme of language. Today, Wisconsin English is increasingly being recognized as a regional dialect here in the United States just like southern English or Boston English or New York English, but it's a surprisingly recent development for Wisconsin (Remlinger et al. 2009) and the Upper Peninsula of Michigan (see fig I.2).

WORDS

Let's shift focus from how people say words to how people make them. (Chapter 5 focuses on words that are distinctively associated with Wisconsin.) How do you say the past tense of the verb *dive*? Many say *dove*, and the strong (irregular) form is so common in Wisconsin that many people are surprised when they hear that other people in our country use the weak (regular) past tense *dived* for this word. In fact, Wisconsin is unusual in having this form of the past tense. Strong and weak past tense forms of verbs are learned when we are very young. We have to learn the past tense and past participle forms for each verb we know. Generally, the past tense in English is formed by adding "ed" to the stem (e.g., I *walked*), and the past participle is formed in the same

FIGURE 1.2. Bumper stickers near the Michigan border outside of Florence, Wisconsin, 2012

way (e.g., *I have walked*). But the original way that Germanic languages like English formed tenses was by changing the main vowel, as in *sing, sang, sung* or *eat, ate, eaten.* So, for example, we say "I get," " I got," and "I have gotten"; in this case, the past participle is made from an irregular past tense form plus the suffix *-en.* The earliest writings in English demonstrate a mixing of these patterns, and that mixing persists to this day. A well-known Wisconsin (but not only Wisconsin) conjugation of the verb *buy* shows this: Wisconsinites can say, "I buy," "I bought," and "I have boughten." Some may bristle at *boughten* but this is simply conjugating *buy* using the pattern we know from words like *get.* All we can conclude when we hear someone conjugate a verb differently than we think it should be is that they grew up in a different speech community than we did. If one has spent their whole life in Wisconsin then it can be a shock to find out that other people conjugate particular verbs like *dive* or *buy* in a different manner. We should understand this difference in the same way that we can understand (but can still feel sorry for) people not from Wisconsin liking the Falcons or the Browns instead of the Packers simply because they grew up in Atlanta or Cleveland.

There are also regional differences in pronouns, like the use of *youse* as in *youse guys*. Although this word really sticks out to many people, when we take a step back it makes perfect sense. Pronouns in English change based on person and number. We mostly have distinct ways of saying singular and plural pronouns, like *I* vs. *we*, *he* or *she* vs. *they*, and so forth, but *you* lacks that: *you* is the second-person pronoun for both singular and plural. If adding *s* marks a plural to a word, why not add *s* to *you* to get a second person plural pronoun *youse*? Of course other kinds of English fill in this gap in other ways, like southern *y'all*, *y'inz* (Pittburghese), or *y'uns* (Appalachian).

Another example of word patterns can be seen in the old Milwaukee stereotype "I'm going to wash my hairs." Most speakers would say "I'm going to wash my hair." The difference in these two examples has to do with the way a speaker treats the noun *hair*; in the first, it is treated as a "count" noun (like *tables*, *books*, etc.) that can be pluralized, whereas in the second it is or treated as a "mass" noun (like *water*, *bacon*, etc.) that cannot be pluralized. As with past tense forms, we learn which nouns are "mass" and which nouns are "count" based on the speech community we grow up in. A final aspect of this particular example (which we'll see more of in a moment) is that *hairs* shows the influence of German immigrants. German treats *hair* (singular *Haar*, plural *Haare*) as a count noun, which provides an idea why it is treated that way in Milwaukee. In fact, while "my hairs" seems to be receding from what we can tell, related patterns are robustly used in the state today, like *a scissors* or *a clipper*.

A final word we should talk about is *warsh* for *wash* simply because it is a very common nonstandard word, not really related to Wisconsin at all (even though we do hear it around here, especially among older folks). This word appears to come to us from the Midlands dialect of American English that runs westward from central Pennsylvania and that expands northward and southward to the area around the Mississippi River.

Phrases

The final part of language that we'll talk about here is how phrases are put together. As we've seen so far, language is extremely systematic at many different levels. Let's start with another example of something that is so common in Wisconsin that people may not understand how interesting it actually is. This is the use of *with* in a sentence like "Are you coming with?" Although this use of *with* is far from unique to Wisconsin, it is not known to many other Americans, for example, in the South or Southwest. Most speakers of American English treat *with* as a preposition, which requires someone or something to complete it. So, a person like that would ask "Are you coming with us?" Or they would substitute *along* and ask "Are you coming along?" Wisconsin speakers use *with* in this instance as something linguists call a "particle." Particles are common in English and everyone uses *up* as a particle in sentences like "Are you going to pick it up?" (English does have some similar expressions that don't require another word with *come*, like *to come to* in the sense of regaining consciousness.) One complexity in the example of *come with* is that whether a verb can use a particle or not is also learned. Thus, just because *with* is a particle doesn't mean that it can be used with all verbs in Wisconsin. Some people who have *come with* also have *bring with*, *go with*, and *take with*—basically any verb indicating motion—while others only have one or two from this list.

We believe part of the reason why *with* can appear as both a preposition and particle here in Wisconsin is that many of the immigrant languages brought to Wisconsin such as German, Dutch, and Danish have their version of *with* as a particle. To put it another way, when immigrants arrived in Wisconsin and began to learn English, they sometimes just directly translated what they wanted to say word by word. If this type of translation gets close enough to work within a community, then this construction will be adopted. We can see this type of effect with a few other words in Wisconsin too. Both the word *yet* and *once* have Wisconsin-specific uses in sentences, such as "Get me a beer *once* as long as you're up *yet*" in Lou and Peter Berryman's folk song "Squirrelly Valley." As in the *come with* example, we believe we can trace these to the language of German immigrants again because a word-by-word translation from German to English produces these types of sentences.

A few other things that one may notice about how English is spoken in Wisconsin are not actually unique to our state. For example, you may notice that you will hear people using double negatives like "I don't like no high heating bills," and although double negatives are definitely looked down on (see chapter 6 about Standard English), you can find people using them throughout the English-speaking world from all walks of life. We also know that earlier forms of English like Old English or Middle English used double negatives in a standard way. In fact, if you believe in following the model of "great writers," then you should use double negatives because Shakespeare did (see chapter 6 for more).

Another often-stigmatized feature is how we conjugate *to be*. "Standard" English has different forms based on the person and number of the subject: *I am, you are, she is, we are, you are,* and *they are* for the present tense and *I was, you were, she was, we were, you were,* and *they were* for the past tense. As with irregular verbs like *get* or *sing*, some speakers use *be* differently. Many people generalize the *she* (third-person singular) form in all cases, so we may hear *I is, you is, she is, we is, you is,* and *they is* for present tense and *I was, you was, she was, we was, you was,* and *they was* for past tense.

Our final example is sentences of the form "The dog wants out" or "The car needs washed," a construction that is moving into Wisconsin from the Midlands area and that is new enough that some of us will have it and some won't. Because of this mix, we can't call it a feature of Wisconsin Englishes yet, but it looks like it will be one in the future. In these types of sentences, verbs like *want* and *need* can be completed with a single word. People who don't have this type of phrase need to say things like "The dog wants to be let out" or "The car needs to be washed."

FINAL COMMENTS

This introduction to some basic features of language and English in Wisconsin should make the remaining chapters much more accessible. Wisconsin presents an amazing opportunity for us to study and learn about how language works. We view this as a great opportunity because by living and working in Wisconsin we can walk outside and be in one of the best laboratories possible. Every time someone learns something about the history of Wisconsin or about a community in Wisconsin it tells us something about language matters in Wisconsin. We hope that you agree that the flip side is true too. When we learn something about the languages spoken in our state, we learn something about Wisconsin. The following chapters lay out a lot of the things we currently know, but you should be able to see that there is much room to improve and add to our knowledge about language and Wisconsin. Please also check the Wisconsin Englishes Project website (http://csu mc.wisc.edu/wep/) to stay on top of new things we learn about Wisconsin and some things we just couldn't fit into this book.

CHAPTER 1

The Native Languages
of Wisconsin

KAREN WASHINAWATOK AND
MONICA MACAULAY

I n this chapter we introduce the native languages of Wisconsin. All
of those still spoken in the state are seriously endangered, yet there
are strong programs in place to preserve and revitalize each one.
Figure 1.1 shows the native population of Wisconsin as of 2010. Figure 1.2 shows the federally recognized tribes of Wisconsin, and as it
makes clear, the state had and still has quite a diversity of native languages. Three language families are represented in the state: Algonquian, Iroquoian, and Siouan. Ojibwe, an Algonquian language, is (or
was) spoken by the Red Cliff, St. Croix, Bad River, Lac Courte Oreilles,
Lac du Flambeau, and Sokaogan bands of the Lake Superior Chippewa.[1] The Potawatomi and the Menominee speak languages related
to but distinct from Ojibwe. The Stockbridge-Munsee represent a
group that came together as they were forced westward and that
includes the Mohekans (also known as Mohegans), the Munsee Delaware, and the Lenape. They no longer speak their native language(s).[2]
All of these—Ojibwe, Potawatomi, Menominee, and the original languages of the Stockbridge-Munsee—belong to the Algonquian family
of languages. The Oneida language is Iroquoian (related to languages
like Mohawk and Cherokee), and the Ho-Chunk language is Siouan
(related to Lakota, Dakota, and Assiniboine, for example).[3] At least
two other tribes were in Wisconsin historically, the Miami and the
Mesquakie (also known as the Fox). Both speak Algonquian languages,

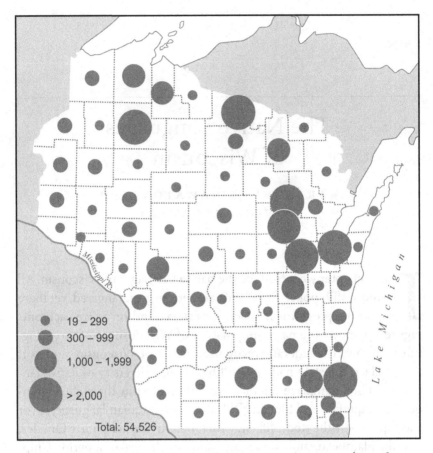

FIGURE 1.1. Native American population in 2010, by county (Data from 2010 U.S. census, table DP-1, "Profile of General Population and Housing Characteristics")

but they were both displaced from their Wisconsin homes and so no longer have a presence here.

Even today, then, Wisconsin's native languages are a diverse set: three Algonquian, one Iroquoian, and one Siouan. The tribes and their languages (and language families) are summarized in table 1.1. Again, all of these languages are either extinct or very endangered. The Algonquian languages of the state have somewhere from zero to maybe twenty-five fluent native speakers each, all elderly. Oneida probably has a few hundred, and Ho-Chunk likewise has a few hundred.

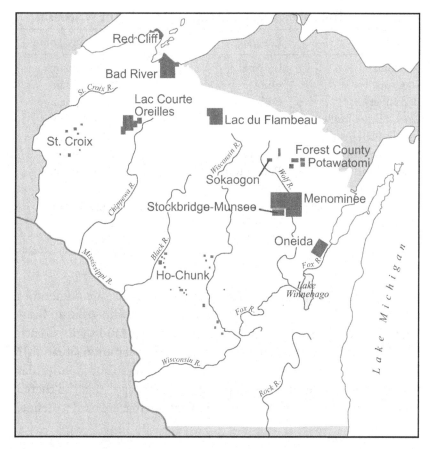

FIGURE 1.2. Tribal areas in Wisconsin (Boundaries have been generalized from geographic data available as 2010 Tiger/Line shapefiles from the U.S. Census Bureau)

WHY DON'T WE KNOW EXACTLY HOW MANY SPEAKERS THERE ARE?

Speaker counts can be done by a community or tribal nation, by linguists, or by the U.S. Census Bureau. Everyone agrees, however, that it is surprisingly hard to do *accurate* speaker surveys. The main problem is that not everybody defines the word *speaker* the same way. Do we mean someone who spoke the language as a first language? Would that include someone who spoke it as a child but hasn't spoken it since

TABLE 1.1. Tribes, languages, and language families of Wisconsin

Tribe / band	Language	Language family
Red Cliff	Ojibwe	Algonquian
St. Croix	Ojibwe	Algonquian
Bad River	Ojibwe	Algonquian
Lac Courte Oreilles	Ojibwe	Algonquian
Lac du Flambeau	Ojibwe	Algonquian
Sokaogan (Mole Lake)	Ojibwe	Algonquian
Potawatomi	Potawatomi	Algonquian
Menominee	Menominee	Algonquian
Stockbridge-Munsee	Mohegan, Munsee, Lenape	Algonquian
Oneida	Oneida	Iroquoian
Ho-Chunk	Ho-Chunk	Siouan

then, having replaced it with English? (Such people are sometimes called "rememberers.") Would we count someone who grew up hearing their parents speak the language, could understand their parents, but always responded in English (actually a very common situation)? With such complexities there's really no clear answer to how one decides whether someone is or is not a speaker of a language—instead there's a continuum with lots of intermediate categories that are hard to define.

What Does It Mean for a Language to Be Endangered?

Just as we can think of who counts as a speaker in terms of degrees, so too can we represent the endangerment of languages on a spectrum. UNESCO commissioned a group of experts to work on the issue, and one of their contributions was the development of a set of nine factors for assessing the robustness of a given language (see Brenzinger et al. 2003 for more details). They stress that their assessment factors should be used together to gain an accurate picture of the status of a language; for our purposes we can just consider the first one: intergenerational language transmission. Table 1.2 provides a list of "grades" for languages based on who in a community uses the language.

TABLE 1.2. Intergenerational language transmission

Degree of endangerment	Grade	Speaker population
safe	5	The language is used by all ages, from children up.
unsafe	4	The language is used by some children in all domains; it is used by children in limited domains.
definitively endangered	3	The language is used mostly by the parental generation and up.
severely endangered	2	The language is used mostly by the grandparental generation and up.
critically endangered	1	The language is used mostly by very few speakers, of the great-grandparental generation.
extinct	0	There are no speakers.

Source: Brenzinger et al. 2003, 7–8.

The premise of this table reflects most linguists' agreement that the crucial question for language retention is whether children are still learning the language; that is, when children in the community are no longer acquiring it as a first language, the language is in serious trouble. You may have experienced trying to learn a language as an adult—undoubtedly you found that it just gets harder and harder the older you get. So if children are not learning a language any more, it's unlikely that there will be fluent native speakers from that generation on, and the chain of natural transmission of a language from one generation to the next will be broken.

WHY ARE THESE LANGUAGES EXTINCT OR IN DANGER OF BECOMING EXTINCT?

Each language has its own set of circumstances, but Stephen Wurm talks about language loss in terms of changes in the "ecology of language" (1991, 2). Wurm points out the similarities to the extinction of plants and animals—something changes in their environment and they are no longer able to survive or thrive. It is in many ways parallel to languages, except that with language extinction the changes in "environment" are generally changes in the cultural and social settings in which the language was previously used. One way the environment in which plants and animals live can be changed is by an invasion by another species that takes over the territory—and that happens with languages too. With Native American languages, of course, the colonization of North America especially by the Spanish, the French, and the British set into motion the cultural and social changes that eventually caused a partial or in many cases a complete shift to Spanish, French, and/or English.

Until recently, government policies not only encouraged such a shift but often mandated it.[4] One such policy, the development of boarding schools for Indian children, played a huge role in the repression of Native American languages and cultures. The first government-run school was the Carlisle Indian Industrial School, founded in Carlisle, Pennsylvania, by Richard Henry Pratt in 1879. Several more were developed soon thereafter; at the height of the program, there were approximately five hundred (see below). The premise was that taking native children away from the influence of their parents and other tribal members and then teaching them to become part of white culture and society would eliminate poverty and other aspects of what was seen as the "Indian problem" in the United States. Pratt is famously quoted as having said, "A great general has said that the only good Indian is a dead one. . . . In a sense, I agree with the sentiment, but only in this: that all the Indian there is in the race should be dead. Kill the Indian in him and save the man" (http://historymatters.gmu.edu/d/4929). In other words, eradicate everything about his or her native culture, including the language.

Imagine the shock and fear these little kids must have experienced— they were forcibly removed from their homes and families and were sent far away to institutions that were run like military schools. Their hair was cut (which was traumatic for those in whose culture it was a sign of mourning and for those who believed that cutting the hair destroyed a person's spiritual power), their clothes were replaced with gender-appropriate uniforms of the times, and they were punished for speaking their native languages. These schools lasted for almost a hundred years, and produced tens of thousands of children who emerged with severe cases of what Amnesty International describes as posttraumatic stress disorder caused by extreme human rights violations (Smith 2007).

Beyond the harm to individuals and community structure, the damage these schools did to the survival of Native American languages is incalculable. When the children went home again, they often found they no longer fit in. They had missed out on an entire childhood of acculturation, including the long process of becoming speakers of the community language. Some were able to regain their footing, but many could not. And many, when it came time to raise their own children, refused to speak their native language to them, speaking English instead. They simply couldn't stomach the thought of their children going through the pain and suffering that they went through. And of course, many of them had been so thoroughly indoctrinated at the boarding schools that they had come to believe their languages were "inferior" in some way.

The state of Wisconsin had its share of government boarding schools (see fig. 1.3): the Tomah Indian Industrial School (1893–1941), the Hayward Indian School (1901–34) and the Lac du Flambeau Indian Boarding School (1896–1906).[5] In addition, religious institutions founded boarding schools for Indian children—for example, the Winnebago Indian Mission School of the Evangelical and Reformed Church, which was founded near Black River Falls in 1878 and moved to a new school building in Neillsville in 1920, and St. Joseph's Catholic School in Keshena, which was opened on the Menominee reservation in 1883.[6]

Wisconsin elders' memories of boarding school vary between appreciation for the sustenance provided (which may not have been luxurious but was sufficient compared to the meager food available at home) to unfortunate memories of another type. One Menominee elder, for example, recalled punishment that resulted in the death of a sibling. The family was never able to achieve closure over the situation, since there were no repercussions for the perpetrator. We also note that children who were sent to boarding schools were trained only for industrial and menial labor rather than for professions that would have provided better pay.

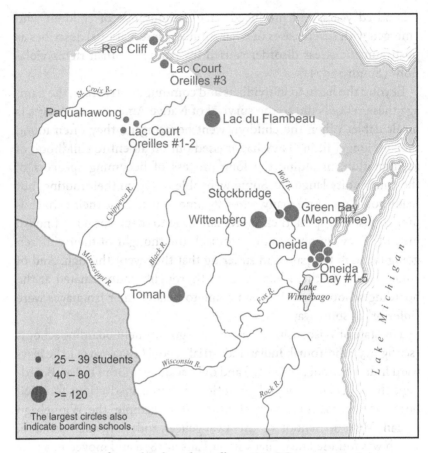

FIGURE 1.3. Indian schools and enrollments in Wisconsin in 1899 (Data from *Statistics of Indian Tribes, Indian Agencies, and Indian Schools of Every Character* [1899])

WHAT CAN BE AND IS BEING DONE ABOUT THE SITUATION?

Native American language revitalization projects are sweeping the nation, and Wisconsin is no exception. Every tribe has language preservation and revitalization programs in progress. The various languages are taught in day care, in schools, and in colleges, and other specialized programs are in place.[7]

If you search around on the web, you'll find that almost every tribe has a website that talks about its language preservation programs. The Ho-Chunk have, for example, an extensive website dedicated to their language.[8] It contains language lessons, as well as audio clips of the language. The mission statement of their language department is an eloquent yet concise statement of the goals of all of the state's language preservation programs: "[This] division is dedicated to ensuring the Hoocąk language continues to be a 'LIVING LANGUAGE.' As a sign of respect to our elders, and the speakers that have come before us, we will continue to speak our language, celebrate our customs, respect the Hoocąk value system and teach our future generations the Hoocąk way of life."[9]

Many tribes also have a tribal body that oversees language revitalization efforts. For example, the Menominee Language and Culture Commission (MLCC) was established by tribal ordinance in 1996.[10] The ordinance requires "that the language be used in tribal business whenever possible, and be taught in all of the schools on the Menominee Reservation—from day care to the tribal college" (Caldwell and Macaulay 2000, 18). The MLCC also regulates and oversees research by outside scholars. Such ordinances are a practical and efficient way of organizing the language work that goes on within a given tribe.

A number of models for language revitalization are being practiced in Wisconsin. Immersion programs are one of the best ways to get kids speaking their heritage language again. It is one of the most promising methods of language preservation because little children have that amazing ability to just soak up language like a sponge. To do successful immersion, the kids have to be in situations (including classrooms or other locations) where nothing but the language in question is spoken. Of course, this means that there have to be enough fluent speakers available to provide the immersion, which can be a stumbling block when there are only a handful of remaining speakers.

Nonetheless, several immersion programs have been started around the state in recent years. For example, in 2007 the Ho-Chunk opened an immersion day care center for children from three months to five years old.[11] From all reports it is going very well, and the kids are picking up the language beautifully—that's what children do. And the Lac Courte Oreilles Ojibwe opened Waadookodaading, an Ojibwe language immersion charter school, in 2001.[12] They have developed their own curricula and are adding grades gradually, as they are able to.[13]

Another popular and successful model is the Master-Apprentice program. In this approach, a master (a fluent native-speaker elder) and an apprentice (a younger person, usually a young adult, who wants to learn the language) are paired in one-on-one interaction. In a very real sense, this model is a form of intensive immersion. The pair spends a predetermined number of hours per day together (usually a half day), speaking only the native language. How exactly these programs work varies a bit, of course, but most are funded by a language preservation grant, and each member of the pair is paid for their time. In an article about the Master-Apprentice approach, Leanne Hinton addresses the potentially controversial issue of paying the participants, noting that "the practical side of the issue is that often this stipend can make the difference between an apprentice who works full time and thus is too busy or exhausted to take full advantage of the program versus an apprentice who can cut back on work hours and devote himself more fully [to the program]" (2001, 219). Ideally, a master and an apprentice are able to work together in the program for three years; at the end of that time, it is hoped that the apprentice will be reasonably fluent and have an extensive vocabulary. Most apprentices go on to become language teachers in the schools and other places where the language is taught in the community. As Hinton says, in many cases the master and the apprentice develop an ongoing relationship, "and the master will also be involved in all the future language activities of the apprentice" (2001, 223).

Language revitalization is a tough road to follow. The sheer amount of work that it takes can be daunting, and participants can get discouraged. But it can also be exciting and exhilarating, and many members of the native communities of Wisconsin are devoting their lives to it. We know a young Menominee man who is speaking only his heritage language to his children, and hearing the first baby-talk Menominee to be spoken in well over half a century is truly inspiring.

NOTES

1. The names can get confusing: what we will call Ojibwe can also be spelled Ojibwa or Ojibway. Chippewa is the Anglicized name for Ojibwe. And the native name for the tribe is Anishinaabe or some variant thereof.

2. They do have some language reclamation projects underway, though— they have decided to focus on Lenape and have started a Headstart immersion school.

3. There are also different names and spellings for Ho-Chunk: sometimes you'll see it spelled Hocąk or Hoocąk—the *a* with a little hook under it represents a nasalized vowel (like in French). They were formerly called the Winnebago, but they have now rejected that name in favor of their own name for themselves.

4. This is in stark contrast to the robust native language opportunities— in the form, for example, of schools and newspapers—that immigrants to Wisconsin enjoyed, as described in chapters 2 and 3.

5. Much of our information about Wisconsin boarding schools comes from Loew 2001; we highly recommend this book for further information on the Native Americans of Wisconsin.

6. The Winnebago Indian Mission School is currently called the Winnebago Children's Home; for its history, see http://www.usgennet.org/usa/wi /county/clark/pinevalley/churches/winnebagoschool/winnebagochildrens home.htm.

7. Even the University of Wisconsin–Madison offers four semesters of Ojibwe, which can satisfy the language requirement for majors in the College of Letters and Science.

8. See http://www.hocak.info.

9. Hoocąk Waaziija Haci Language Division, http://www.hocak.info/my site/HTM%20All/Mission%20Statement.html.

10. See http://www.menominee-nsn.gov/MITW/cultureCommission.aspx.

11. See http://www.hocak.info/mysite/HTM%20All/Wahooceg%C4%AF kra%20-%20Daycare.html.

12. See http://www.waadookodaading.org.

13. A very nice video of Ojibwe language revitalization programs, including Waadookodaading, can be found at http://www.tpt.org/?a=productions&id=3.

CHAPTER 2

Older Immigrant Languages

FELECIA LUCHT

In the early to mid-1800s, waves of European immigrants reshaped and added new complexity to the already rich linguistic landscape that diverse populations of Native American inhabitants had created, bringing many other languages and varieties of languages with them, including German, Norwegian, and Dutch. In isolated rural areas, small towns, and growing urban areas, immigrant settlers built close-knit communities in which their languages and dialects were used on a daily basis at home and in the public sphere. Over the following decades, gradual societal changes triggered a shift in language use, favoring English, as these communities became more integrated with the largely English-speaking environment. Despite the dominance of English, however, one can still find communities in Wisconsin today in which these older immigrant languages continue to play a role in family life, festivals, and celebrations. And as discussed in subsequent chapters (particularly in chapter 5), these languages have helped shape Wisconsin Englishes, and their influence can still be found in the speech of almost all Wisconsinites.

Wisconsin in the nineteenth century was frontier territory, sparsely populated and rich in natural resources. Attracting immigrants to Wisconsin was seen as key to cultivating the land and building a base for economic growth and development. Wisconsin experienced its first big population boom in the early to mid-1800s. From 1836 to 1850, the population of Wisconsin grew by 2,514 percent, beginning with a population of 11,683 in 1836 and increasing to 305,390 by 1850 (Smith 1973, 466). In 1850, approximately one-third of Wisconsin's population was foreign born; these immigrants primarily came from German-speaking countries, Scandinavian countries, and Great Britain and Ireland (Nesbit 1989, 148, 151; Ostergren 1997, 152–53).[1] Despite this dramatic population growth, large areas of the new state were still being made available for settlement, which was the impetus for the creation of the Office of State Commission of Emigration in 1852.[2] Using pamphlets translated into various languages and newspaper advertising, this organization sought to inform immigrants about Wisconsin and provide advice on settlement to immigrants, as well as give tips on avoiding fraud while making the journey to Wisconsin (Strohschänk and Thiel 2006, 95, 103). More and more European immigrants kept arriving in Wisconsin, many to join their families and friends who had already settled in the state. Robert Ostergren (1997, 155) notes that the "old immigration" continued until 1880, when a wave of "new immigration" began, drawing more immigrants largely from southern and eastern Europe, including Italians, Poles, Czechs, Slovaks, and Russians. As shown in figure 2.1, by the year 1900, the majority of the state had a foreign-born population of over 15 percent. In Milwaukee and in the northern part of Wisconsin, some areas were over one-fourth or one-third foreign born.

Many early settlements were predominantly "homogenous ethnic and Yankee communities" (Smith 1973, 464). Even in urban areas like Milwaukee and Madison, ethnic neighborhoods and wards developed, as immigrant groups tended to congregate with others who shared the same heritage, culture, and language. Linguists often use the term *speech island* (from German *Sprachinsel*) to describe these immigrant communities, as the immigrant language was the primary language used in communities largely surrounded by English-speaking communities. To varying degrees, urban and rural immigrant communities were in contact with speakers of other languages, particularly English. Despite being in contact with English speakers, these communities still were largely able to function using the immigrant language in many areas of their daily lives—at home, in educating their children, when

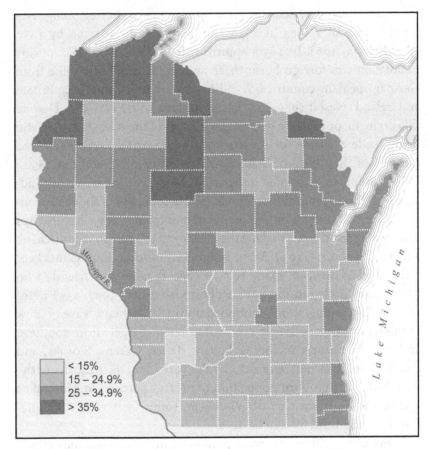

FIGURE 2.1. Percentage of foreign born, 1900, by county (Data from the 1900 U.S. census. On this map and others that use county data from 1900, Rusk and Menominee counties had not been established. Rusk was founded in 1901. Menominee, established in 1959, appears in many early maps as the Menominee Reservation.)

they attended religious services and celebrations, when they communicated with the neighbors, and even in local business interactions.

Although they were never completely isolated from their environment, these immigrant communities had strong local autonomy, were relatively self-sufficient, and relied primarily on the local economy for survival. In rural communities, the local economy was usually heavily based on family farms, which provided for families and the immediate community. In urban areas, immigrant settlements often had access to businesses operated by members of the same ethnic community. Miranda Wilkerson and Joseph Salmons (2008, 271) provide examples of jobs held by German monolingual speakers in four townships (Hustisford, Germantown, Kiel, and Sheboygan) as reported in the 1910 U.S. census. They worked as teachers and clergy, merchants and salespeople, as well as stonemasons, tailors, painters, carpenters, contractors, and cheese makers. That is, in 1910, it was apparently possible to hold a wide range of jobs and play a wide range of roles in the community, even if you couldn't speak English.

Immigrant communities often gathered socially for cultural events, offering opportunities to immigrants to use their native tongue with their neighbors and friends. Concerts provided venues in which to hear tunes from the homeland and sing familiar songs. Many communities formed musical organizations and bands. The Lebanon Band in Lebanon, Wisconsin, for example, continues to bring neighbors and families, sometimes several generations of the same family, together.[3] Theater also played a role in many of these early immigrant communities. The first Czech drama in the United States is said to have been performed in the town of Kossuth in Manitowoc County (Rechcigl 2005, 194). As detailed by Peter Merrill, the theater played a significant role in immigrant Milwaukee, offering German-speaking immigrants the chance to see European German productions, popular plays translated into German, and, to a lesser degree, German American plays (2000, 33).

Ethnic religious institutions played a role in maintaining language use in the community. The Lutheran churches of Lebanon, Wisconsin, for example, served as a bastion of German language use up until the 1960s and 1970s (Lucht 2007). Some churches, however, were multiethnic from the start. Italian immigrants in Cumberland, Wisconsin, attended Catholic church services with other immigrant groups in the area prior to founding an Italian congregation (Andreozzi 1987, 112). In the early days of many of these communities, prior to the founding of public schools, religious institutions were also often the providers of education.[4]

Wisconsin was home to a lively immigrant language press, which allowed its residents to keep up with events in the state and at home in

their native tongues (see fig. 2.2). Owing to its large German population, the German American press had a firm footing on Wisconsin
soil. In 1890, when the number of German American newspapers published in Wisconsin had reached its peak, there were a total of eighty-
nine (Salmons 2002, 183). But other immigrant groups also had their
own papers. In his *Guide to Wisconsin Newspapers* (1958), Donald
Oehlerts lists papers published from 1833 to 1957, including in German, Norwegian, Swedish, Bohemian (Czech), Polish, Danish, Dutch,
Slovenian, Yiddish, Italian, French, and Hungarian. The lifespans of
immigrant newspapers varied, and many immigrant language newspapers, like other smaller papers of the time, folded after short publication periods. But there were also immigrant language papers that
continued for several decades, such as the Polish-language weekly
papers, *Rolnik* (*The Farmer*), published in Stevens Point from 1892 to
1960 (Oehlerts 1958, 205), and *Kuryer Polski* (*Polish Courier*), published
in Milwaukee from 1888 to 1962.[5] There are even a few immigrant language newspapers still in circulation today, such as the *Gwiazda Polarna*
(*Northern Star*), a Polish-language biweekly published in Stevens
Point. Founded in 1908, the *Gwiazda Polarna* gained readers as other
Polish-language papers folded and was once heralded as "the largest
Polish-language weekly newspaper in the United States" ("Bartosz Era
Is over at 'GP'" 1973).

In addition to newspapers, other materials were published in local
publishing houses that catered to the immigrant communities. One of
the first editors of the Wisconsin-based Czech newspaper, for example,
also printed dictionaries and grammar references (Rechcigl 2005, 194).
A literary culture also thrived, as immigrant writers created poems,
prose, and plays. In *Other Witnesses*, Cora Lee Kluge provides biog-
raphies of and samples of work by German American writers. Kluge
stresses the importance of immigrant language literature to recogniz-
ing the contributions of different ethnic groups in the development of
American history and culture and in allowing insight into non-Anglo
perspectives on issues of the day (2007, xi–xii). One controversial
issue in the mid-1800s in Wisconsin was that of prohibition. During his
time in Milwaukee, publisher and playwright Christian Essellen wrote
a play titled *Bekehrung vom Temperenzwahn* (which roughly translates

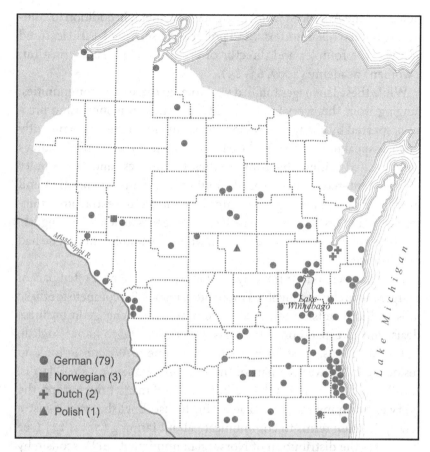

German (79)
Norwegian (3)
Dutch (2)
Polish (1)

FIGURE 2.2. Locations of select foreign-language weekly newspapers in 1900 (Data from *Guide to Wisconsin Newspapers, 1833–1957*, compiled by Donald E. Oehlerts. The data include only newspapers extant in 1900.)

as *Conversion from the Temperance Mania*) in which two of the main characters publicly support the ban of alcohol but drink regularly in private (Kluge 2007, 4–5). Kluge notes that the play not only pokes fun at the hypocrisy of temperance laws but also does not feature any Anglo-American characters, demonstrating the independence of the German American community at that time (2007, 6). Kluge also cites the example of Mathilde Franziska Anneke, publisher of the *Deutsche Frauen-Zeitung* (German Women's Newspaper) and proponent of civil rights and the American women's rights movement. In addition to composing poetry, religious texts, and political prose, Anneke also lectured and was the founder and director of the Milwaukee Töchterinstitut, a women's academy (2007, 83–85).

While these languages fulfilled vital roles in these early communities, ranging from the everyday to the literary, there was increasing pressure, spurred by changes in society, to assimilate to the predominantly English-speaking culture. In the early years, most goods and resources were located within the communities themselves, and community life was centered on the local community. But with urbanization and modernization came a greater interdependence on extracommunity resources and organizations, which created spaces for speaking English, and often required the use of English, where the immigrant tongue had once sufficed.

Jobs that were once primarily local in nature were now often part of a larger hierarchy and involved more bureaucracy. To compete for these jobs and jobs outside of the local community, to engage in business deals, and to expand one's business, it became vital to know English. In the late 1800s, most Norwegians who came to Wisconsin took up residence in the western part of the state and worked on small farms. But Richard Fapso notes that to buy land and market their crops, the Norwegian immigrant found it useful to use English, even if just a few agriculture terms to communicate about farming (2001, 24) (see fig. 2.3 for the distribution of Norwegian immigrants in Wisconsin by county). He goes on to state that many Norwegian immigrants lacked the resources at first to have their own farms and often started out working for Yankee farmers, which required some use of English, even if just the new terms and practices they needed in this foreign environment (24–25).[6] Samples of jobs reported in the 1850 and 1930 U.S. censuses for the small town of Lebanon, the city of Watertown, and the large city of Milwaukee reveal that jobs in 1930 reflect increasing urbanization (to varying degrees) and increasing specialization and that more of them, including factory-related jobs and jobs created through advances in communication and transportation, were connected to larger bureaucracies and extracommunity organizations in comparison to those in 1850 (Lucht, Frey, and Salmons 2011, 361).

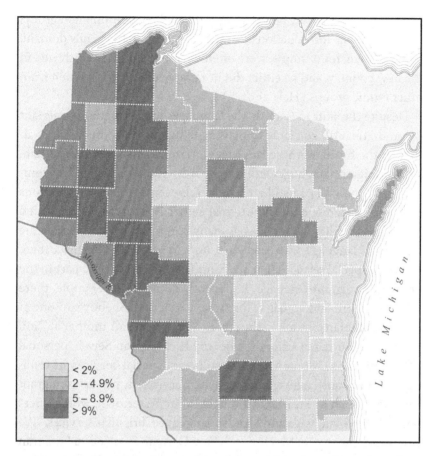

FIGURE 2.3. Percentage born in Norway, 1900, by county (Data from the 1900 U.S. census)

Publications in the native tongue of the communities were now no longer available or being published by publishing houses outside of the communities, which often preferred to invest in English-language publications that would have wider appeal and, more to the point, were more economically viable in the changing market. Religious materials first available in the native tongue became more readily available in English.

Early immigrant groups tended to marry others of the same group, which helped preserve the immigrant language. But in smaller immigrant communities, finding a partner from the same ethnic background was harder, and so they began to marry outside their immigrant group, which led to the introduction of another language in the family domain. Swedish men, for example, were often unable to find a Swedish wife in the new country, and so either did not marry or married women from other ethnic groups (Hale 2002, 35).

Despite the shift to English, the languages of the original immigrant communities still continue to play an active role in some families, although the future of these languages as family languages is uncertain. The immigrant languages still often have symbolic value in the communities, and one can still attend church events or local celebrations that feature elements of the original settler immigrant communities. Even though religious services in many communities where once the immigrant language was used have now gone over to English, there are some special services that are conducted in whole or in part in the original immigrant language. As recently as 2011, for example, there were two German-language Christmas services in Sheboygan: one at Trinity Lutheran Church in the city of Sheboygan and another at Zion Evangelical Lutheran Church in nearby Kiel (Alyson Sewell, personal communication). Some churches still hold special services in traditional immigrant languages along with services in newer immigrant languages, such as St. Mark's Evangelical in Watertown, which offers both German-language and Spanish-language Christmas services.[7] We also see this change in Manitowoc's First German Evangelical Lutheran Church, which started out as a German-language church and now has regular Hmong-language worship services.[8]

We also still find traces of these immigrant languages in the songs of the ethnic festivals held throughout the state today. In describing the ethnic festivals in Milwaukee, "*the* city of festivals," Victor Greene (2009, 286, 288) explains how the festivals were used both to show appreciation for cultural diversity and to facilitate assimilation into American culture.

Even though these older immigrant languages may no longer be actively used in their respective communities as they once were, there are still many speakers of older immigrant languages living in Wisconsin today, as seen in figure 2.4.

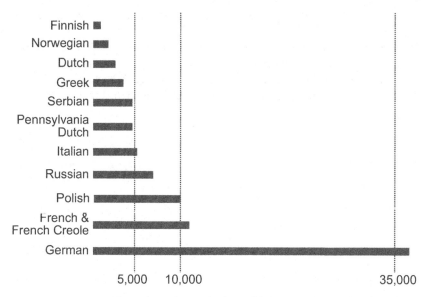

FIGURE 2.4. Number of speakers of select older immigrant languages in Wisconsin, 2006–8 (Data from the American Community Survey 2006–8)

NOTES

I would like to thank Miranda Wilkerson for her discussion of ideas for this chapter.

1. This chapter refers to these immigrant groups by nationality and ethnicity to provide a general picture of immigrant groups, but it is important to remember that within these groups there are often diverse cultural groups, regional affiliations, religious groups, and multiple languages used and that individuals can have multiple ethnicities. This is explored by Deborah Padgett (1989, 31) in her study of Serbian immigrants in Milwaukee and discussed in Ostergren 1997, 154.

2. For a thorough discussion of the creation and mission of the Wisconsin Commissioner of Emigration, see Strohschänk and Thiel 2005.

3. See http://townoflebanon.com/lebanon_band.

4. For more information on education in early immigrant communities, see chapter 3 on Wisconsin's German schools.

5. See the *Kuryer Polski* Indexing Project, http://www.pgsa.org/kuryerpol ski.php.

6. Haugen 1953 provides the classic treatment of Norwegian in the Midwest, including the roles English played in the community at various times.

7. See http://www.lambstolions.com/thelionspride/?p=3831.

8. See http://www.firstgerman.org/First%20German/history.htm.

Immigrant Languages and Education
Wisconsin's German Schools

ANTJE PETTY

In the second half of the nineteenth century, the Wisconsin landscape was dotted with public, private, and parochial schools where
children and grandchildren of immigrants were taught in German,
Norwegian, Polish, or other older immigrant languages that are described in chapter 2. Today, the language of instruction in Wisconsin
schools is almost exclusively English, but the state still has large immigrant communities with families who speak Hmong or Spanish (chapters 8 and 9), and the question of how to teach immigrant children is
as current as it was 100 or 150 years ago. While the languages have
changed, basic issues remain: Should Wisconsin children be taught in
English only, in their native tongue, or in a bilingual setting? How important is the language of instruction for "quality education" and content
learning? What role does the school language play in the integration,
acculturation, and "Americanization" process? And how important is
the language spoken in the classroom for the maintenance of ethnic
identity and cultural heritage? This chapter explores the example of
schooling among German-speaking immigrants and their descendants
in Wisconsin, the largest non-English-speaking population in the state's
early history.[1] Education patterns in some other language communities
such as Norwegian or Polish were generally similar, although the populations were smaller populations.[2] Still smaller groups, though, such as
West Frisians, who numbered only a few hundred, lacked institutional

support and infrastructure like church services or a press and did not have schools teaching their language.

As detailed in chapter 2, the numbers of settlers in Wisconsin—first Yankees from the eastern states and later European immigrants— increased rapidly in the mid-nineteenth century. German-speaking Europeans came to the state in three large waves. The first significant wave arrived in the early 1850s from southwestern German states such as Bavaria, Württemberg, Hessen, and the Palatinate, as well as the German-speaking regions of Switzerland and the Austrian Empire; a second wave, which originated mostly in the northwestern and central German states of Westphalia, Prussia, and Saxony, came after the Civil War; and the last and largest group of German-speaking immigrants arrived from the northeastern German lands of Pomerania and East Prussia in the 1880s (see fig. 3.1).

The timing was fortuitous: in the early 1850s, at the same time when many southwestern Germans were planning to leave their homeland, the young state of Wisconsin was eager to increase its small population. Southwestern Germans, mostly small farmers, craftspeople, and merchants, who sold their property at home to acquire land in America, filled the bill. In addition, a number of intellectuals fled the failed revolutions of 1848–49 and came to America hoping to implement their political and social ideas there (see fig. 3.2 for the distribution of German immigrants in Wisconsin by county).[3]

To lure emigrants who might otherwise have gone to other U.S. states, Brazil, or Canada, the state of Wisconsin launched an all-out recruitment effort, establishing the Wisconsin Office of Emigration, a state agency that from 1852 to 1855 tried to influence potential emigrants' choice of destination even before they had left their home country. This agency also had an office in New York; representatives there would meet arriving immigrants who might not have yet decided on a place to settle. To attract immigrants, the Wisconsin Office of Emigration published advertisements in German papers and distributed pamphlets and posters—all in German—that boasted of Wisconsin not only as the state with the cheapest land, the best geography, climate, soil, waterways, and the greatest supply of timber and other natural resources but also as a state fostering religious and political freedom, where "the

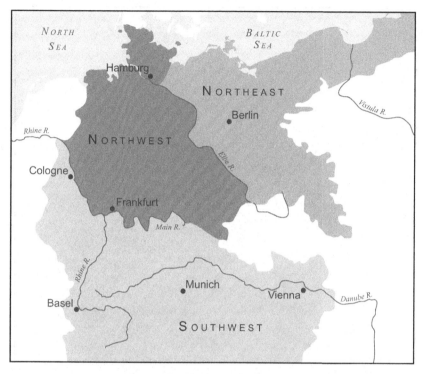

FIGURE 3.1. Central European origins of German-speaking immigrants to Wisconsin (Based on maps by Wisconsin Cartographer's Guild 1998 and König 2007)

immigrant can keep his old nationality as long as he wants to . . . and, after one year, has the same political and voting rights as the native" (Wisconsin Staats-Einwanderungs-Behörde 1853, 2) (see fig. 3.3).

The publications point out that as of 1853 already one-third of the Wisconsin population had come from German lands and that "the significant number of Germans already living here, especially in the more populated areas, has contributed greatly to the establishment of a real German life style and the continuation of the traditions from the fatherland. . . . German music, song, theater, and educational societies can be found in many places. . . . Yes, [Wisconsin] will be a new German Fatherland. Right in the middle of America, it will become a second happy homeland." Furthermore, "free public schools and an

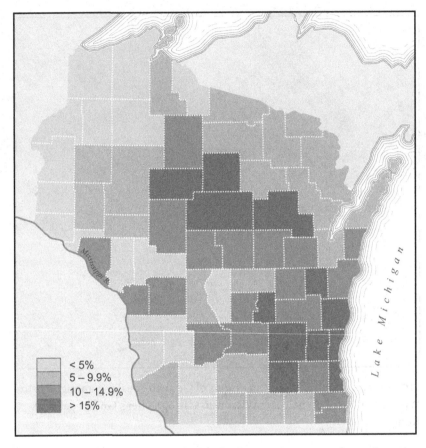

FIGURE 3.2. Percentage born in Germany, 1900, by county (Data from the
1900 U.S. census)

educational system of the best kind will be provided for" (Wisconsin
Staats-Einwanderungs-Behörde 1853, 3, my translation). Between 1867
and 1887 and once more from 1895 to 1901, the agency (later called
the "Wisconsin Board of Immigration") again took up the recruitment
effort.[4]

The propaganda of the Office of Emigration played directly to the
concerns and priorities of these emigrants, and once in Wisconsin, one
of the first actions new German settlers took was to establish schools.
Back in the German states, seven years of school attendance had been

Wisconsin.

* * *

Bevölkerung, Bodenbeschaffenheit und Klima im Norden Wisconsin's.

Handbuch zum Nutzen und Besten der Einwanderer.

Erste Auflage.

Herausgegeben

von der

Staats-Einwanderungs-Behörde.

Mitglieder der Behörde.

Wm. H. Upham, Staats-Gouverneur, ⎱ ex officio.
Henry Casson, Staats-Sekretair, ⎰

Henry L. Besse, James J. Nelson, Ole Larson.

Henry L. Besse, Präsident. G. W. Bishop, Sekretair.

FIGURE 3.3. Booklet in German by the Wisconsin Board of Immigration, ca. 1895 (Courtesy of the Max Kade Institute for German-American Studies at the University of Wisconsin–Madison)

mandatory since the eighteenth century—in Wisconsin, seven years of at least twelve weeks per year became mandatory only in 1879. In Germany, the literacy rate was high, education was held in high esteem, and big strides had been made in pedagogy and academic teaching from early childhood to university education. Now the German settlers tried to replicate the schools they had become used to while at the same time taking advantage of the organizational freedoms they found in America.

Most German American children went to public schools. While no comprehensive record of school attendance or language use exists for the early decades of public education in Wisconsin, community publications, state superintendent reports, and personal accounts paint a vivid picture. In rural German communities during the early settlement years, especially in grade schools, public school instruction was mainly in German. Teachers were hired from Germany, and German-language textbooks were first imported and later published in the United States. The Wisconsin School Law of 1848 had stated that "the population of a school district can decide to have other languages taught in connection with the English language," but it did not specify the language of instruction (Wisconsin State Legislature 1848, 247). A new law in 1854 required that all "major subjects" (without specifying which) should be taught in English. However, since schools were under local control and locally financed, state education laws in these early years had an advisory character and were not enforced, and individual school districts determined their own language of instruction.

In later years, different arrangements developed. For example, families from Württemberg and Hanover, who founded the district school in the town of Honey Creek in Sauk County in 1855, arranged for the first four years of instruction to be exclusively in German. Between 1859 and 1885, "winter school" was taught in English for five months of the year, while "summer school" was taught in German for two months. After 1885, English became the language of instruction all-year round, while German was taught as a language class one hour a day (Jacobi-Dittrich 1988, 150–51).

English-speaking families who found themselves in the minority in German communities often learned and used German and sent their children to German public schools. Sometimes this led to conflict, as for example when a few Yankee families in Herman, Dodge County, complained to the state superintendent in 1851 that their district school teacher "did not talk plain English" and that their children deserved an "English school and not a forked tongue one" (Jacobi-Dittrich 1988, 124). This particular teacher was replaced for a different reason, but another German-speaking teacher was hired, and it is not known where the Yankee children in question subsequently attended school. On the other hand, Balthasar Meyer, who was born in 1866 in Mequon, Ozaukee County, and went to an English district school for a few years before he attended a German Lutheran school, remembers: "We talked German at home. The trouble [in the district school] was with the language. We had Irish teachers who knew no German and German pupils who knew no English. The Irish families represented by children in school all understood German and their children could talk German. German was the language of the playground. We learned English words, but did not know their meaning" (Jacobi-Dittrich 1988, 159). In other districts—for example in Addison, Washington County, in 1852—there was debate over what books in what language should be purchased for the school library (Jacobi-Dittrich 1988, 127–28).

In general, evidence suggests that the language question was worked out at the community level and that German instruction had a significant role in public education—sometimes for decades after immigration—if there was a critical mass of German-speaking families. For example, in his annual report on the 1863 school year, the superintendent of Ozaukee County, which was largely settled in the 1840s, wrote (Horn 1864, 624):

Not a little trouble and difficulty I had to encounter in many districts where the people desired to have an exclusive German school, or where such school should be kept a portion of the time. You are perhaps aware that nearly one-third of the districts in this county are peopled exclusively with Germans, while in the other districts, with one here and there an exception, the Germans outnumber the other inhabitants by nine to one. All applications for the employment of such [German-speaking] teachers . . . I have made dependent upon the unanimous

wish of the people in the district, after being satisfied that the applicant
was otherwise qualified.

In Milwaukee, with a large German-speaking population (one-third
were German born in 1867), most German American children went
to public school. German parents favored having their language taught
in the public schools, but they were even more interested in the im-
provement of public education and were represented on the district
school boards. They were concerned with overcrowding, shortage of
equipment, and the limited number of subjects taught, as well as the
shortage of trained teachers. In Milwaukee's early years, many teachers
with a formal education had been trained in Germany. In the following
decades, education initiatives developed at the city level contributed sig-
nificantly to the establishment of requirements for state-wide teacher
certification, the implementation of educational standards and mandatory school attendance, and the addition of subjects such as biology,
geography, art, music, and physical education to the curriculum. While
the teaching of German was also important to German parents, German never became the language of instruction in Milwaukee public
schools. In 1857, the school board passed a resolution that required the
hiring of German-language teachers in all schools "where the need for
German education was felt," and in the late 1860s, another resolution
stated that German-language classes must be offered as an optional subject in all schools. This proved to be popular with Milwaukee families.
As late as 1899, 73 percent of all students in the Milwaukee public
school district (including many children who did not have a German
background) took German as an optional subject (Goldberg 1995, 178).
    Some German families in Milwaukee (mostly businessmen and bet-
ter-educated immigrants) were looking for a more academic education
and more German instruction for their children than the public schools
provided. In 1851, they started a *Schulverein* (education society), and
in 1853, the German-English Academy, a bilingual school with a broad
curriculum and a focus on natural sciences and hands-on and inquiry-
based learning, in which all subjects were taught in both languages,
was founded. Other such schools opened in the city, but even during
their peak year (1867), these schools combined had not more than a

thousand students out of the more than twenty-two thousand school-age children in the city of Milwaukee that year (Pomeroy 1867, 158).[5]

Advancing the education of children, however, demanded improving the education of teachers. In 1866, the state of Wisconsin opened its first four normal schools, but many German Americans, especially in Milwaukee, wanted more. Thus in 1878, a group of German American teachers from around the nation—including those involved in the founding of the German-English Academy—established the National German-American Teachers Seminary in Milwaukee, which strove to provide American schools with well-trained teachers who could teach all subjects in both German and English.

Parochial schools offered another option for German-speaking Americans in nineteenth-century Milwaukee. In 1867, the city had three German Catholic schools and seven German Lutheran schools, all following a traditional faith-based curriculum. Together they served about three thousand students. Instruction in these schools was in German and in English, with generally more German in the Lutheran schools than in the Catholic schools.

Parochial schools were even more popular among German Americans in the countryside, particularly where no German instruction was available in the district schools.[6] In fact, the parochial schools—especially the Lutheran ones—often maintained German the longest, sometimes into the mid-twentieth century.

Over the course of the nineteenth century, Wisconsin's Catholic Church and Lutheran synods established their own German-language school systems. Catholic schools were mostly run by nuns with teaching experience who in the beginning had come from Germany but who were later recruited from among the Sisters of St. Dominic in Racine and the Sisters of St. Francis in Milwaukee. The Lutheran synods, after initially importing teachers from Europe, eventually also established their own teaching academies in the Midwest, of which Northwestern College in Watertown was the most prominent in Wisconsin. Here young men were trained to become teachers and pastors.

While many students attended an all-German parochial school for the entire school year, others joined (mostly) English public schools in the winter and only attended German parochial schools in the summer.

1907

Zeugnis
— der —
Evang.-Luth. Friedens-Schule,
— zu —
MENOMONIE, - - WISCONSIN.

für .... Frieda Hörcig ....

Erklärung: { 100 bedeutet ausgezeichnet. 80 bedeutet gut. Unter 70 bedeutet ungenügend.
90 = sehr gut. 70 = befriedigend.

	April	Mai	Juni	Juli	Aug.	Sept.	Oct.	Nov.	Dez.	Jan.	Feb.	März
Betragen =		92				98	95	90	96	96		98
Aufmerksamkeit =		97				98	98	98	98	98		98
Fleiß = =		99				95	100	96	98	99		99
Fortschritt = =		98				98			98			99
Tage gefehlt =										3		
Zu spät gekommen												
Vor Schluß entlassen												
Katechismus =		100				99	100	98	100	100		100
Biblische Geschichte =		92				90	95	95	98	95		98
Rechnen = =		96				96	96	95	95	96		96
Deutsch = =		100				97	100	100	96	98		100
Englisch = =		97				95	95	95	94	96		96
Schönschreiben		87				85	84	85	85	85		85
Geographie =		90				90	100	90	95	95		93
Geschichte = =												

Unterschrift der Eltern:

Büchergeld:

Unterschrift des Lehrers:

In Freistadt, Ozaukee County, a town founded in 1839 by immigrants from Pomerania and considered the oldest German settlement in Wisconsin, Trinity Lutheran Church School served both as a parochial school (in the morning) and district school (in the afternoon), an arrangement that seems to have lasted at least into the 1870s. According to G. R. Brueggemann's church history (1964, 69), "The morning at school was devoted to religion, German, reading, and Arithmetic. In the afternoon English was studied, and the children were strongly encouraged to speak English outside the classroom. High German [standard German] was spoken in the school; however, Plattdeutsch [Low German] was the language spoken in the homes of Pomeranian families, and on the school playground."

In the second half of the nineteenth century, there were many rural communities in Wisconsin whose population largely spoke only German, often in the second or even third generation after immigration, and whose community members could speak both German and English but still preferred to conduct their personal and business life in German. A resident of Lebanon, Dodge County, claimed that in the late 1880s "very few of the second generation understand a word of English" (Jacobi-Dittrich 1988, 161), and in 1910, in Hustisford, Dodge County, U. S. census data and other community documents still identified almost a quarter of the population as monolingual German speakers—more than fifty years after major German immigration to the town had ceased (Wilkerson and Salmons 2008).

In some instances, speakers of German were resented by Anglo-Americans, who blamed the German private schools, particularly the parochial schools, for the stubborn holdouts and "backwardness" of German-speaking communities in Wisconsin. Complaints began to surface in the 1860s, such as in this 1864 report from the Fond du Lac County superintendent for public education (Cundall 1865, 23–24):

A part of the localities of foreign population, especially German, very unwisely as it seems to me, withhold their children from English schools and send them to German schools. In one day I visited three schools containing 11, 4, and 3 pupils respectively, and yet these districts draw public money on 498 scholars. The children were in German schools! Their love for their vernacular is commendable, and yet it is plain that the German schools thus patronized are a great detriment to the public schools. They ought to retain their language, since a man who can speak two languages is worth two men; but the interests of the State demand a law requiring the presence of all children under a certain age in Public School until they shall have mastered the rudiments of an English education.

In the 1870s and 1880s, as anti-immigrant sentiment grew throughout the country, the call for "Americanization" and education in English grew stronger. In 1889, the Wisconsin legislature passed a law introduced by Dodgeville assemblyman Michael Bennett (Republican), which among other things included more stringent requirements for school attendance and stated that "no school shall be regarded as a school, under this act, unless there shall be taught therein, as part of the elementary education of children, reading, writing, arithmetic and United States history, in the English language" (Wisconsin State Legislature 1889, 729–33). The purpose of the law was ostensibly to set higher education standards across the state, as expressed in the *Madison State Journal* in 1890:

> The Bennett Law was conceived by American patriotism to protect and bless the poor boy by assuring him the largest advantages of citizenship, especially by affording him, if the son of foreign parents, an equal chance in life. . . . It is American patriotism to provide that every child born in the land shall have one of the chief attributes of an American— a knowledge of the language of our people. . . . It is American patriotism . . . to demand that no boy, however obscure, shall grow up ignorant of the universal laws of communication in this land; that tongue in which the laws are written that govern him.[7]

German Americans, Norwegian Americans, and other immigrant groups, however, were incensed. They interpreted the Bennett Law as an affront to their culture, their language, and—since by 1889 most German and Norwegian instruction occurred in parochial schools— their religion. They considered themselves as American as any other citizen and felt their patriotism questioned on the basis of their ethnic background and the language they spoke. In fact, many a father or grandfather had fought earlier in the American Civil War, in some cases in entirely German regiments. They also resented the notion that a German-language education was inferior to an English-language education in public schools or that their children were assumed to be "poor" and disadvantaged in America simply on account of their language. Last but not least, remembering the time when immigrants were promised free expression of their culture and language in Wisconsin, they now saw an infringement of their basic American freedoms. In the end, Wisconsin's ethnic populations banded together: the Republican Party was voted out of office in 1890, and the Bennett Law was repealed the same year.

But what was it like for a German American child to go to school in nineteenth-century Wisconsin? Learning Standard German was the first challenge for most children. At home, many of them spoke German dialects, often radically different from the German taught in school, and for many children learning to read, write, and speak Standard German meant learning a foreign language. This was expressed by a Pomeranian Low German speaker born in 1903 in Hamburg, Marathon County:

> Most of [us here] spoke Low German, but some also spoke High German [standard German]. And when we went to school, most of our pastors came from Germany, and they spoke High German, . . . but all the people in the neighborhood spoke Low German. When we used to go to summer school, then we had to speak High German. We weren't used to that at home and were always trembling in school when we had to answer [the teachers]. For that reason I decided that my children shouldn't have to go through that, so I spoke High German with them, but nowadays the summer school and religious instruction are all in English.[8]

Thus children who went to bilingual schools or English winter schools and German summer schools not only had to learn two new spoken languages but also had to deal with two different scripts. German books were printed in the old *Fraktur* style (often called "Gothic" type in English), while English texts were published in roman type. Writing was even more challenging. For compositions in German, students had to learn a form of the old German script—a way of writing that is so different from the modern version that it is unintelligible for most native speakers of German today—while English texts had to be written in modern cursive.

Educators responded to these challenges, and teaching materials were produced in America specifically for American German-language schools. Many examples can be found in the library and archives of the Max Kade Institute for German-American Studies at the University of Wisconsin–Madison and some can be seen on the institute's website (mki.wisc.edu). Primers for first graders frequently included both languages as well their print types and scripts, such as that shown in figure 3.5, a page from *Witter's Deutsch-Englische Schreib- und Lese-Fibel* (1905), here introducing the letter G. There were special exercise books to learn the German script, such as *Krone's Deutsche Schulvorschriften*, published in the late nineteenth century.

Different types of schools published different textbooks in accordance with their teaching philosophies. The textbooks of parochial schools focused on moral upbringing and church doctrine and included Bible passages, prayers, and hymns. The teaching materials for the secular, private German-English schools reflected their founders' ideals of "inquisitiveness, tolerance, and a free spirit." Here the German literary classics dominated language instruction; biology and earth sciences were taught with hands-on methods in the field; and music, theater, art, and physical education were integral parts of the curriculum. German-language classes in public schools, especially in the 1880s and 1890s, were often seen by school authorities as the best way to reach new immigrant children and turn them into good American citizens, and the German texts used in public schools reflect this goal in their focus on American themes, history, and values.

Whatever the type of school, textbooks were proudly written for Americans by Americans. For example, when the letter *F* and the word *Fahne*, meaning "flag," are introduced in *Das ABC in Bildern* (*The ABC in Pictures* [ca. 1905]), the drawing shows an American flag (see fig. 3.6).

𝒢 𝑔 𝒢𝑢𝑟𝑡𝑒𝑛 **Garten.**
garden.

𝔊 𝔤 G g

Da ift ein Garten. Adele ift im
There is a garden. Adele is in the

Garten. Albert, haft du einen
garden , Albert, have you a

Garten? Geh' in den Garten!
garden ? Go into the garden.

Der Griffel ift hart. Gold ift gelb.
The slate-pencil is hard. Gold is yellow.

*Haft du den Garten! Gold
ift gelb. Jenny ift artig.*

FIGURE 3.5. Page from a first-grade reader used in German American schools, 1905 (Courtesy of the Max Kade Institute for German-American Studies at the University of Wisconsin–Madison)

E e

Ernſt und Elſa und Erneſtine
Freuen ſich am Wippen,
Singen luſtig alle drei,
Doch es giebt ein
Mordsgeſchrei,
Wenn ſie einmal kippen.

Fahneſchwingend grüßt
das Fränzchen,
Guter Schneemann, dich;
Auf den kahlen Kopf
ſetzt Flora
Dir den Hut noch mütterlich.
Nun kriegſt du keinen
Schnupfen,
Schneemann, bedanke Dich.

F f

FIGURE 3.6. Page from *Das ABC in Bildern*, alphabet book for German American children, ca. 1905 (Courtesy of the Max Kade Institute for German-American Studies at the University of Wisconsin–Madison)

Math problems in the 1870 *Arithmetisches Exempelbuch* use examples from the American world, such as addition questions that ask how many dollars a merchant has spent on his wares. And the *Viertes Lesebuch für die deutschen katholischen Schulen in den Vereinigten Staaten von Nord-Amerika* (*Fourth-Grade Reader for German Catholic Schools in the United States*) published in 1874 includes texts in German on cities "in unserem Vaterland," which means "in our fatherland," from Baltimore to Milwaukee, as well as a five-page story on the newly established "national park in the territories of Montana and Wyoming" (Yellowstone National Park, established in 1872), which proudly concludes with "Thank you to Congress, which made this park the property of our nation and [provided a place] where we hope many people will find time to relax and improve their health" (*Viertes Lesebuch* 1874, 298–302, my translation).

At the turn of the twenty-first century, 42.6 percent of Wisconsinites claimed "German" as their primary ancestry, but less than 1 percent spoke German at home (U.S. Census Bureau 2000) (see fig. 3.7).

Anti-German sentiment during World War I has often been blamed for the demise of the German language in America, for the disappearance of German schools, and the decline of German-language instruction. Indeed, in Milwaukee's public schools enrollment in German classes dropped from thirty thousand students in 1917 to twelve thousand students in 1918 after anti-German propaganda began, and in 1919, all foreign-language instruction (not just German) was banned from city elementary schools. In 1917, the German-English Academy felt pressure and changed its name to Milwaukee University School. Several years earlier, however, it had already dropped its bilingual teaching model and was offering German only as an optional language class. World War I–era anti-German reactions thus only accelerated a process of language decline that was already well under way (Nollendorfs 1988, 184).

Immigrant languages often do not survive into future generations, especially if there is no continuing immigration. They may last longer in homogeneous rural settlement areas and in tight-knit ethnic city neighborhoods, but eventually they disappear there, too.[9] By 1919, more than one generation after the last major wave of German-speaking

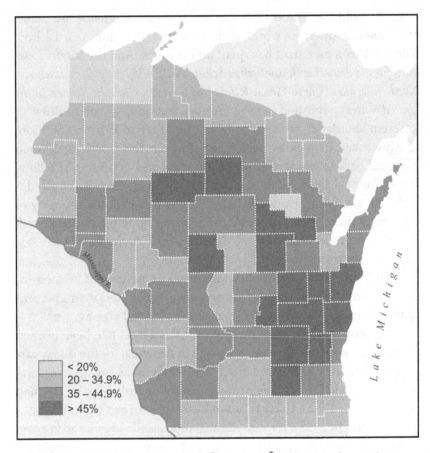

FIGURE 3.7. Percentage reporting German as first ancestry in 2006–10, by county (Data from American Community Survey 2006–10, table B04001, "First Ancestry Reported")

immigrants had arrived in Wisconsin, most German Americans in urban areas had assimilated to such a degree that they did not insist on German education for their children anymore, even if they still spoke German at home and in their clubs and churches and still read German papers and books. Furthermore, already two decades earlier, teachers who taught in bilingual programs and programs in which German was an option (such as in the Milwaukee public schools) noticed differences among their pupils with a German background: those who were fluent speakers, on the one hand, and those who benefited from "formal grammar and translations" like the Anglo-Americans, on the other (Toth 1990, 73–76). Nevertheless, despite anti-German sentiment in the rest of the country, many parochial schools in rural Wisconsin continued to teach at least part of their curriculum, summer school, or Sunday school in German, in some cases until the 1940s. In this environment German Americans were often bilingual, but the German language continued to be central to the fabric of local society.

The history of German schools in Wisconsin reminds us that education in immigrant languages has a long tradition here. It refutes the myth that immigrants in the past immediately gave up their native tongues in favor of English and casts doubt on the notion that instruction in languages other than English or bilingual instruction is of lower quality. The German American experience also shows that it takes a critical number of people as well as certain community structures and dynamics to keep ethnic cultures and languages alive. The role of the German language in the larger community established the basis for its use in schools. Still, those who had hoped that formal school instruction in and by itself would help maintain German among second- and third-generation German Americans were disappointed to see it give way to English. Nowadays, there are no longer substantial groups of children in Wisconsin who speak German at home. When German is taught in Wisconsin schools today, it is neither to support language maintenance nor to maintain ties to a community's heritage but to enrich the education of monolingual English-speaking children and to introduce them to cultures other than their own.

NOTES

1. In 1890, at the height of German language presence in the state, 519,000 Wisconsinites (31 percent of the population) were foreign born, half of them hailing from German-speaking countries (U.S. Census Bureau 1890).

2. Small Norwegian Lutheran schools were scattered around the countryside and dominated education in many Norwegian American rural settlements in Wisconsin (such as Koshkonong, Muskego, and Trempealeau), in some cases to the end of the nineteenth century (Paulson and Bjork 1938, 76). One example in the Polish American community is Sacred Heart Polish Catholic

Parish and School in the town of Polonia in Portage County founded by Polish immigrants between 1872 and 1874. Until the mid-1890s, five Franciscan Sisters from Cracow, Poland, taught children from Portage and neighboring counties in Polish, while one American teacher provided English as a second language instruction (Goc 1992, 50–51). The use of Polish in the school and church services was slowly phased out, and by 1950, Sacred Heart had dropped the Polish language completely (Goc 1992, 136).

3. In 1848, popular uprisings led by students, intellectuals and workers spread through the thirty-nine German states. The revolutionaries opposed the aristocracy and fought for representation, German national unity, living wages, and freedom of the press, assembly, and religion. By 1849, however, their efforts had failed, the existing autocratic structures remained in place, and many disillusioned participants left Europe.

4. A detailed account of the first "Wisconsin Office of Emigration" can be found in Strohschänk and Thiel 2005.

5. According to the superintendent's report of that year, 9,424 students were enrolled in public schools and 6,429 in private schools. Since not all enrolled students actually attended school, the daily attendance rate in all city schools was estimated at 52 percent. In 1869, Milwaukee had twenty public schools (grades 1 through 9), one public high school, and thirty-seven private schools (Pomeroy 1869, 107).

6. In Norwegian American communities, Lutheran schools that provided instruction in Norwegian predominated. Norwegians who chose parochial over public schools gave three main reasons: the parochial schools taught in Norwegian (unlike in early German settlements, Norwegian teachers were rare in public schools), they provided religious instruction, and the quality of education offered by them was far better than that offered by the public schools. Lutheran schools dwelled on the high quality of the teaching in order to attract those Norwegian families who were otherwise tempted by the "free" public schools. According to Koshkonong resident A.C. Preus, writing in the Norwegian weekly *Emigranten* in 1858, "To secure good schools it is not enough to have good laws, good school buildings, and plenty of money. . . . The most important thing is to have good teachers. . . . No external advantages can make a poor teacher into a good one and therefore a poor school into an efficient school. Now throughout the whole West where the Norwegians have settled I am acquainted with the condition of the American schools, . . . and I maintain without reservation that in general they are as bad as it is possible for them to be and still deserve the name of schools. Why? Because nine out of ten teachers are totally incapable of conducting a decent school. For the most part the teachers are young people who themselves are just out of school—perhaps a few years too soon—often lacking in knowledge, but more often lacking in those qualities which are necessary for guiding and teaching a group of children. . . .

If the school were able to retain these young people . . . , they could perhaps through experience and diligence improve and become useful teachers. But . . . rarely does a teacher remain for more than one term—that is, from three to six months. . . . Let it be said that one occasionally finds really capable teachers, and sometimes we are fortunate enough to have Norwegians who are able to conduct an English school. But as long as we see it in the hands of thoughtless timeservers, . . . we regard it with fear and suspicion and do not send our children there. For a bad school is worse than no school at all" (Paulson and Bjork 1938, 76–77).

7. A clipping of this article can be found in the Wisconsin Historical Society Library Collection, Bennett Law Scrapbook, 1889–90.

8. The interview was conducted by Jürgen Eichhoff on June 18, 1968, and is located in the Max Kade Institute North American German Dialect Archive, EIC 20. The region was settled by immigrants from Pomerania in the late 1860s, and the dialect is spoken in some homes still today.

9. Exceptions are cases in which the language is integral to a religious community, as in the cases of Pennsylvania Dutch in Old Order Amish communities and Yiddish in Hasidic communities.

CHAPTER 4

The Non-Wisconsin Sound
of Southwest Wisconsin

KRISTIN SPETH

T he English of southwest Wisconsin is unique and has been almost since English speakers first came to this part of the state. If we compare the local speech of, say, Mineral Point to that heard in Green Bay, Milwaukee, or Rhinelander, we notice different pronunciations and phrases such as *warsh* for *wash* and *they was* for *they were*, identified in the introduction as not typical for current Wisconsin English. What makes the dialect in this corner of the state so different? Interestingly, southwest Wisconsin has historically included not one but two dialects that are unique in Wisconsin: a Cornish English dialect that was spoken early on as a result of heavy immigration from Cornwall, and a dialect normally found south of Wisconsin that has come to be spoken here owing to geographic and immigration factors linking southwest Wisconsin culturally and economically with areas outside the state. In this chapter, we'll see features of the distinctive, non-Wisconsin dialects spoken here and consider how this transition took place.[1]

Any discussion of southwest Wisconsin history has to include the Cornish. Cornwall is the southwestern corner of England, and the Cornish dialect is the type of English spoken there, not to be confused with the Cornish language.[2] The southwest corner of Wisconsin saw a wave of Cornish immigrants between 1830 and 1850, mostly miners interested in the lead deposits to be found there, and it is said that these

Cornish immigrants shaped the dialect of English still spoken in the region. Figure 4.1 shows the two towns most of the immigrants came from, Redruth and Camborne, as well as three features of speech characteristic of this region: *thee* (or *'ee* or *ye*) for *you*, loss of initial *h-* resulting in *'ouse* instead of *house*, and the past tense form *catched* instead of irregular *caught*.

We know from local history and census records that the Cornish were not the first English speakers in southwest Wisconsin. There were earlier settlers from other parts of Britain and from elsewhere in the United States, all bringing various dialects of English. However, the Cornish were the first English-speaking group to live in this area permanently in relatively large numbers, and the Cornish dialect has been

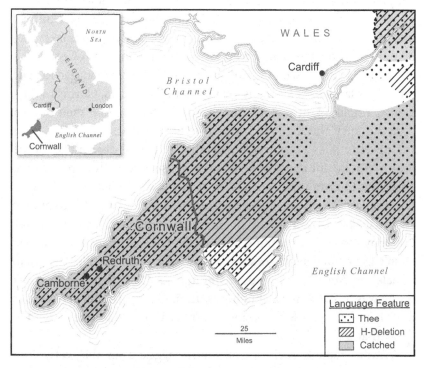

FIGURE 4.1. Origin of settlers of Mineral Point, Wisconsin, relative to regional language features in Cornwall and southwest England (As discussed in Upton and Widdowson 1996)

popularly considered to be much more influential on the later speech of the area than other, less well-represented dialects, such as Irish English or some kind of American English.[3] When groups such as Norwegians and Germans came to Mineral Point, they would have heard the English spoken by their Cornish neighbors and could have easily acquired it from them—Cornish English learned as American English.

Local historian Louis Copeland offers an important early look at Cornish immigrants. At the time of his writing in the late nineteenth century, there were still many immigrants in the area, as well as their children who had grown up speaking the immigrant dialect. According to his description, the dialect of Cornwall was unique among varieties of English, so much so that understanding the Cornish dialect, with its "odd words" and "peculiar pronunciation," could be difficult; he goes so far as to say, "It is quite impossible for a stranger fully to understand a conversation carried on by typical Cornish miners, i.e., by miners who have changed little since emigrating from Cornwall."[4] As chapter 2 explains, immigrant groups in Wisconsin managed to hang onto their languages for many years; by similar means, Cornish immigrants, a tightly knit social group, were able to maintain their dialect, even though it was hard for outsiders to understand.

Copeland does not provide a detailed technical description of the accent, but he does note several words in use among the Cornish that give clues to pronunciation, as well as many words that are noticeably nonstandard American English. Besides terminology specific to mining (the main profession among the Cornish immigrants), we find many everyday words. If something was excellent, it was *braav*, and a person wasn't bold but *bould*. To show respect for older people, call them "Uncle" or "Aunt," and friends are *my dears*. A Cornish miner wouldn't say he was from Cornwall, but he *wor* from *Carnwell*. Later generations must have heard these terms and pronunciations, and some learned to speak that way.

Written accounts such as Copeland's suggest a sizeable, early population of Cornish English speakers with a unique dialect that could have influenced the speech of later immigrants. In recordings from a later period, we still hear some of these features. In the 1940s, Helene

Stratman-Thomas recorded many interviews with residents in Cornish settlement areas as part of her research on Wisconsin folk music, recordings full of family histories, descriptions of Cornish American life, and jokes and stories told in the "Cornish dialect." Most of these interviewees are only one generation removed from Cornwall; the storytellers are the grown children of Cornish immigrants. The stories and jokes are told in a language that the audience would understand as representing Cornish.

Dialect features are often used for effect in telling jokes and stories. These features make up the act of telling a joke, along with comic timing and tone of voice.[5] As the children of Cornish immigrants heard these tales, they would also learn the language that went along with them. In these recordings, therefore, we hear features connected to the dialect. Not all of these features were used by every speaker or by every speaker consistently. Also, most are not unique to Cornish English; loss of initial *h-*, for example, is heard in a wide range of English dialects, and double negation is found in essentially all dialects of English.

The following exchange between two friends was recorded in Dodgeville, Wisconsin:

'Ello, Carrie. 'Ow are ye today?
Tarrible. A bit tired today, for a girl my age.
Well, Ah aren't tired at all.[6]

We see here some of the common features of these Cornish stories: *ye* or *'ee* for *you*, loss of *h* at the beginning of words, and pronunciations such as *tarrible* for *terrible* and *Ah* for *I*.

The Cornish tendency to drop *h-* at the beginning of words got its share of laughs, as in the following story:

I'll tell you a little incident about a son who had been away to school, came back and was just a little embarrassed by the persistence of his parents in leaving off their *H*s where they really belonged and putting them on where they did not belong. So, his father was talking about ham and of course he called it *'am*.' The son said, "Father, you mustn't say ''am.' You say ''AM.' And "No," the father says, "well I did say ''am.'" "Oh, no," the son says, "you mustn't say it that way," he says, "you say ''AM.'" And the mother was amused, and she says, "They both think they're saying ''am.'"[7]

In the Stratman-Thomas recordings, we hear all three features represented in figure 4.1—loss of *h-*, *'ee* for *you*, and the past form *catched* instead of *caught*. Other interesting verb forms include double negation as in *nobody couldn't*, use of *s* on present tense verb forms that have no ending in most kinds of English, like *I says* and *you knows*, and the specific verb form *I ben't* for *I'm not*. The sound *t* could attach to a following word: *'tis* (=*it is*), *a t'all* (=*at all*), *a t'ome* (=*at home*), *t'other* (=*the other*). Sometimes a preposition marked the speaker as Cornish, for example, using "to" where standard American English uses "at" (*all to once, to home*). Some sentences used different constructions altogether, such as *Make 'ome the door* for standard *Shut the door*. And vocabulary was sometimes distinctly nonstandard: a Mineral Pointer could be *grizzling* ("laughing") or *wisht* ("sad") or *click hand* ("left handed") or even *screeching like a witnick* ("screeching like an owl"). The next chapter considers words used throughout Wisconsin, but these Cornish English words are rarely used outside southwest Wisconsin. Not all of these phrases are in common use anymore, but they are still understood by some people in this area—even though I grew up in Wisconsin, I had no idea what a *witnick* was until some friendly residents of Mineral Point told me.

These stories were recorded about one hundred years after the Cornish immigrated to the area. The storytellers had learned the dialect features mainly from older relatives and used these features when telling stories to add local and ethnic color. Time had apparently not eliminated these Cornish dialect features, at least in the context of storytelling, a kind of performance.

Recordings made after 1950, even with older speakers, do not use identifiably Cornish features. Instead, we hear another dialect that is unusual in Wisconsin—the regional American dialect often called "Upper Midlands." Upper Midlands is spoken in a belt running roughly south of Wisconsin that includes the cities Des Moines, Iowa; Peoria,

Illinois; and Canton, Ohio.[8] What could account for this switch in dialect? Chapter 2 notes how early immigrants tended to cluster together and later generations dispersed and came into contact with other dialects of English. Over time, southwest Wisconsin saw similar social shifts, leading to a redrawing of dialect lines. Settlers moved in from other countries and from elsewhere in the United States, bringing their versions of English with them. Cornish was no longer the main (or sometimes only) type of English that children heard. Just as Norwegian and Irish Americans, for example, lost most of the features that sound clearly Norwegian or Irish, so Cornish Americans lost the ethnic features of their language. There is still a strong sense of Cornish heritage in the region, but it is no longer clearly heard in the speech by the measures investigated here. An earlier ethnic immigrant dialect has instead been replaced with a regional American dialect spoken in nearby areas.

So Cornish Americans now sound American and not Cornish, but why didn't they end up sounding more like other Wisconsinites? The introduction to this volume has laid out how geographic boundaries (the Wisconsin River) and transportation routes (Highway 18) can become social and therefore dialectal boundaries. These borders link southwest Wisconsin with northwest Illinois. Northwest Illinois and southwest Wisconsin already shared similar immigration histories, since both areas were settled heavily by the Cornish. And lead mining was a major occupation in both northwest Illinois and southwest Wisconsin early on, resulting in economic ties that southwest Wisconsin did not share with the rest of (mostly agricultural) Wisconsin. Geographic, transportation, ethnic, and industrial lines all led to strong communication with northwest Illinois, so we can see how this corner of Wisconsin would be tied linguistically with Illinois rather than with other parts of Wisconsin. (See chapter 10 for more on the interplay of language and geography.)

In figure 4.2 showing current dialect boundaries, we can see how southwest Wisconsin is linguistically distinct from the rest of the state. To the north, Wisconsinites speak the dialect called "North Central," and to the east "Inland North." Mineral Point and neighboring towns, however, use Upper Midlands, along with northwest Illinois and southern Iowa.

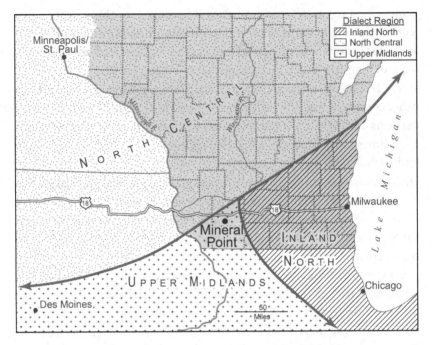

FIGURE 4.2. Mineral Point relative to major cities, and dialect regions and isoglosses in Wisconsin and the Upper Midwest as determined by the Telsur Project at the Linguistics Laboratory, University of Pennsylvania (www.ling.upenn.edu/phono_atlas/maps/MapsIN/TelsurIN.html)

The Wisconsin State Historical Society houses recordings of interviews conducted with residents of southwest Wisconsin from the 1950s to the 1980s. Some of the people interviewed are descendants of Cornish immigrants, and others grew up in the same area. Most of these recordings are personal histories, not stories, so we do not hear the storyteller's Cornish style.[9] But even in the more natural speech of these later recordings, we hear local characteristics that are unusual in Wisconsin English, though they are found elsewhere in the United States where Upper Midlands is spoken.

The following description of daily life comes from a resident who was born around 1900 and was recorded in August 1966 in Mineral Point:

Why, work all through the week eight hours a day, from eight to five, and then, uh, Saturdees they'd quit at noon, and they'd go home and have their dinner, and warsh and change and come downtown in the saloon. And there they was. And then they'd—they'd get into arguments with one another and come out in the street and fight her out. Knock each other one down. I've heard of them fighting all the way down the street. Knock one down, the other fellow would get up and maybe knock the other one down.

We hear in this recording three nonstandard features: *Saturdee, warsh,* and *they was. They was* is a construction found in many dialects (see chapter 6), though it is not usually considered to be typical of Wisconsin speech. The other two features are rare in Wisconsin and are clear markers of Upper Midlands, in which *Saturday* and other days of the week can be pronounced with *dee,* and an intrusive *r* often shows up in *warsh* for *wash* (Allen 1973–76, 293, 299). (Young people in Mineral Point tell that they still hear older generations say *Warshington.*)

A couple generations ago it was more common to hear some of these noticeably different features, such as *they was. Wh-* at the beginning of words is pronounced as [ʌ], that is, with the *h,* so that *which* and *witch* are pronounced differently. The *wh-* pronunciation is used in several dialects, though it's thought to be receding over the generations, but in Wisconsin it appears to be confined to the southwestern corner. A more unusual feature is *l* pronounced almost like a low vowel, so that *cold* sounds like *cowd* or *code.* The vowel in *toe* is sometimes pronounced like the vowel in *too* (*goopher hole* for *gopher hole, soocial* for *social*). Just as in the earlier recordings, we hear *t* attaching to following words: *a t'all* (*at all*), *a t'any rate* (*at any rate*). This might be a holdover from the Cornish English dialect, or it could be a shared feature—it is certainly common to many English dialects, including in the American South and the Mid-Atlantic.

A casual visitor to southwest Wisconsin might not notice anything striking about the language, since Upper Midlands as a dialect can be hard to pinpoint. Its features are not as noticeable as, for example, a stereotypical Chicago accent, and Midlands could, according to William Labov, Sharon Ash, and Charles Boberg, "claim to be the lowest common denominator of the various dialects of North America" (2006, 263).[10] Nevertheless, a keen observer will hear sounds and words that stand out from general Wisconsin speech.

The two dialects as represented in Helene Stratman-Thomas's collection from the 1940s and the Wisconsin State Historical Society collections from the 1950s through the 1980s do not share many of their most distinctive linguistic characteristics with each other. Rather than an unbroken continuation of a dialect, we see two separate dialects spoken in the area at different times: first Cornish English, then Upper Midlands. The differences in these two dialects, so clearly heard in the recordings, show us how dramatically English in southwest Wisconsin has changed over the last 150 years, as all languages do naturally. Immigration history, geographical boundaries, and shared culture and trade have linguistically separated Mineral Point and nearby towns from the rest of Wisconsin. The speech of this area was once distinctive in the state in its use of Cornish English, and it remains so today with the Upper Midlands dialect, something rare in Wisconsin.

NOTES

1. For general information on the dialects of Wisconsin and dialect theory, see Allen 1973–76; Labov, Ash, and Boberg 2006; Millar 2008; and Trudgill 2004.

2. For more on the Cornish dialect in Wisconsin, see Copeland 1898 and Jewell 1990.

3. Linguists refer to this situation as a "founder effect"; see the case studies provided by Millar 2008 and Trudgill 2004, among others.

4. Copeland (1898, 323) lists several words that came from Cornwall; the words cited here are found on pages 322–23. For a more recent history of the Cornish in Wisconsin, including a description of Cornish English spoken in Wisconsin, see Jewell 1990.

5. Leary's *So Ole Says to Lena: Folk Humor of the Upper Midwest* (2001) provides an interesting account of dialect in folk humor, as well as several Cornish American jokes.

6. Helene Stratman-Thomas Collection, CD no. PMU 316, track 1, Mills Music Library, University of Wisconsin–Madison. Stratman-Thomas's interviews from the 1940s are available on compact discs held in the collection.

7. Helene Stratman-Thomas Collection, CD no. PMU 322, track 2.

8. See Labov, Ash, and Boberg 2006 for details about American dialects, including Upper Midlands. Allen 1973–76 also has helpful dialect information going back a couple generations.

9. Some of the most interesting stories can be heard in the following recordings (the examples in this chapter are also found in these recordings): interviews by Holzhueter 1982, Rannells 1985, and Schereck 1955 and interviews with Neal 1955, Simpson 1953, and Tyrer 1966.

10. Labov, Ash, and Boberg go on to note, "Many features of the Midland are the default features—that is, the linguistic landscape remaining when marked local dialect features are eroded" (2006, 263).

CHAPTER 5

Words Used in Wisconsin

LUANNE VON SCHNEIDEMESSER

When my daughter was a freshman in college, studying in the state of Washington, she called me one night and told me she had said to friends that they should go buy some bakery. She explained, "Everybody laughed at me. What's wrong with that?" Nothing is wrong with that, except location. While many people use this term in Wisconsin to mean the pastries or baked goods bought in a bakery, for most people in the United States the bakery is only the *building* where sweet rolls and breads are sold.

I am the senior editor for the *Dictionary of American Regional English* (*DARE*), a project housed at the University of Wisconsin–Madison for which we have studied the lexicon of speakers of American English throughout the country and written about it in a five-volume dictionary recording not only regional but also folk speech.[1] In the course of this work we have shown many words to be what I call Wisconsin words. But not all of them are labeled as Wisconsin words. *Bakery*, for example, in the sense "baked goods, esp sweet baked goods," is labeled *chiefly Ger settlement areas*. In Wisconsin you can go into many bakeries, some in grocery stores, and see signs announcing "Fresh Bakery." But not in the state of Washington.

This chapter discusses words used in Wisconsin English. Many terms still used today came with early immigrants groups, discussed in chapter 2. Other terms of course originated in English. And as has been said

elsewhere in this volume, language changes. Our stock of words continues to develop: some are added, some are changed, and some are
lost. Some of the words used in Wisconsin are used only in part of the
state. I'll give examples of all of these aspects of language change.

One point should be made clear at the outset, however: whether we
say Wisconsin words or words used in Wisconsin, we mean the latter.
They are used in Wisconsin, but usage of words does not usually stop
at state borders. Wisconsin has a system of trunk roads, but evidence
for use of *trunk* in this sense can also be found in neighboring states,
as well as scattered usage in California and Nebraska, for example (see
fig. 5.1).[2] Usage of the term *sweet soup*, a fruit soup, is shown by DARE
to be largely confined to the Upper Midwest and Wisconsin, the areas
where large numbers of Scandinavian immigrants settled. Both terms
are Wisconsin terms, even if not used exclusively in Wisconsin.

WORDS FROM IMMIGRANT LANGUAGES

The introduction to this volume reproduces the famous "Hill map,"
which attempts to represent the ethnic makeup of the state of Wisconsin around 1940. This geographical pattern has not changed greatly
for these ethnic groups: Kazimierz Zaniewski and Carol Rosen say
that "even today the geographic patterns of ethnicity in Wisconsin are
remarkably distinctive, and the state remains a place where the association between ethnicity and place is strong" (1998, xv).

The Germans were the largest group of immigrants to Wisconsin
(see chapters 2 and 3). In 1990 over 45 percent of the Wisconsin population, roughly 2.2 million people, claimed German ancestry (Zaniewski
and Rosen 1998, 73). The immigrants at first spoke German in the
communities where they settled (most heavily in eastern Wisconsin
but also in central and southern Wisconsin); with time and more interaction with their non-German neighbors, however, they slowly switched
to English (chapter 2). But their English retained terms from German, which their neighbors also picked up, and which spread, many
widely in the country: *sauerkraut, kaput, coffee klatsch, borrow* 'lend',
dummkopf. Others remained closer to home, in all or part of the German settlement areas: *pfannkuchen* 'pancake'; *pfeffernuss* 'a highly spiced

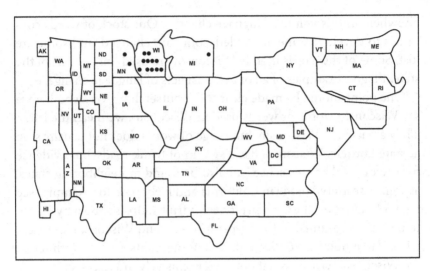

FIGURE 5.1. Locations of respondents reporting *trunk* (Reprinted by
permission of the publisher from *Dictionary of American Regional English*,
vol. 5, *SI-Z*, edited by Joan Houston Hall [Cambridge, MA: The Belknap
Press of Harvard University Press, 2012], 728, copyright © 2012 by the
President and Fellows of Harvard College)

Christmas cookie'; *rutschi* 'slide, slip'; *sauerbraten* 'a dish of beef mari-
nated in a solution with vinegar'; *schnibble* 'a small piece or scrap'; *hand
cheese* 'cheese formed into balls using one's hands'; *oma* 'grandmother'
and *opa* 'grandfather'; and *once* used in an emphatic or limiting way,
such as *Come here once!* (see the introduction). And a few are used
or known mainly in Wisconsin.[3] *Bratwurst* 'fried or grilled sausage, usually made of pork', has very wide usage in Wisconsin; the term started
in areas of heavy German settlement but is especially frequent in Wisconsin. Johnsonville Sausage Co. in Johnsonville, Wisconsin, sells its
products to every state in the union now, so usage has spread with the
product. The shortened form *brat*, however, is Wisconsin. The first
day I was in Madison, I saw a sign on State Street for the "Brathaus."
Although I speak fluent German, when I saw the sign I thought of *brats*
with the vowel in *cats* (transcribed as /bræts/), meaning "unruly small
children," and wondered what kind of a place this Madison was. I never
associated it with *bratwurst*. I quickly became familiar with *brats* with

the vowels in *cots*, /brats/, and *bratfests*, as all citizens of Wisconsin are.[4] *Schafskopf* and its translated English form *sheepshead* is a most popular card game in Wisconsin (see figs. 5.2 and 5.3).[5] *Halt's maul* (politely translated "be quiet" or "shut up") is said to be known in Wisconsin, although I have never heard it in an English context. People who use the phrase *from little on* (or *up*), meaning "since childhood, from the time one is little or small," have looked at me in amazement when I tell them that it is a translation of a German phrase, *von klein auf* (or *an*).

Some phrases or words are carried on in families without knowledge of where they came from (not just words from German but also from other languages). Mary, a woman from Janesville, asked if *schnibble* was a real word. Indeed it is, deriving from the German *Schnippel* 'a scrap, a small piece'. She uses the term with her grandson, who doesn't speak German but addresses her as "Oma." Another phrase I'm trying to find out more about—it has been mentioned a few times by people

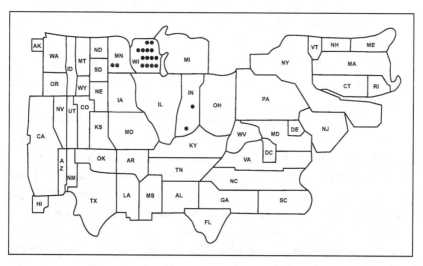

FIGURE 5.2. Locations of respondents reporting *sheepshead* (Reprinted by permission of the publisher from *Dictionary of American Regional English*, vol. 4, *P-Sk*, edited by Joan Houston Hall [Cambridge, MA: The Belknap Press of Harvard University Press, 2002], 895, copyright © 2002 by the President and Fellows of Harvard College)

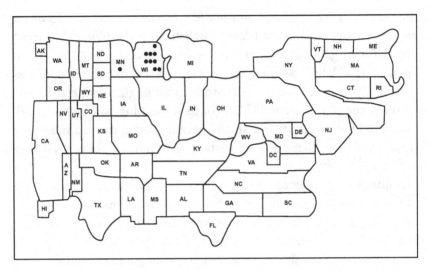

FIGURE 5.3. Locations of respondents reporting *schafskopf* (Reprinted by permission of the publisher from *Dictionary of American Regional English*, vol. 4, *P-Sk*, edited by Joan Houston Hall [Cambridge, MA: The Belknap Press of Harvard University Press, 2002], 780, copyright © 2002 by the President and Fellows of Harvard College)

I've met—is *(s)he doesn't belong to Marshall*, or *Manitowoc*; this is also a translation from German, meaning that the person is not originally from that area.

Ancestry from other immigrant groups that settled in Wisconsin is claimed by far fewer people (as is also true for the United States as a whole). The second largest ethnic group in Wisconsin is the Poles, with 325,320 people claiming Polish ancestry in 1990 (Zaniewski and Rosen 1998, 109). Many of the contributions of the Polish to Wisconsin English consist of food items, a common happening, since the immigrants imported their culture from the homeland, including foods. *Czarnina* 'a type of duck's blood soup', *golumpki* 'stuffed cabbage leaves', *kielbasa* 'a type of pork sausage', *kishka* 'a kind of blood sausage', *paczki*, pronounced *poonchkey* and *punchkey* 'a pre-Lenten filled doughnut' (or what you may call a *bismarck*) are a few of them.[6]

Following behind the Poles are the Norwegians, the third largest ethnic group in Wisconsin, with 257,345 people (Zaniewski and Rosen

1998, 134). These immigrants settled originally mostly in southeastern and south central Wisconsin and then migrated to the western part of the state. Some of the terms taken over into Wisconsin English from Norwegian (some of them also from Swedish and Danish) include *lutefisk* 'dried (cod)fish soaked in lye' (you may have to *water out* the lutefisk) and *lefsa* 'flatbread made from potatoes', *bakkels*, also *sandbakkels* and *fattigmanns bakkels* 'a type of cookies or pastry', and *julebukk* and its English translation *Christmas fool* 'costumed or disguised people who call on neighbors between Christmas and New Year and receive food and drink'. While it can be found throughout Scandinavian settlement areas, especially Wisconsin, and is more Danish than Norwegian, the *kringle* 'a sweet large usually oval or ring-shaped pastry often with fruit or nut filling' is especially known in the city of Racine. Towns such as Stoughton and Westby, with many people of Norwegian ancestry, celebrate Syttende Mai, May 17, Norwegian Constitution Day (the constitution was signed on this date in 1814) or the National Day of Norway. *Ish* and *ishy* are terms used most frequently in Minnesota but may also be heard in Wisconsin instead of *ick* and *icky*. *Uff da*, another term that can be used as an expression of disgust—or of surprise—can be heard in Minnesota and Wisconsin and other places of Norwegian settlement.

Other non-English-speaking ethnic groups also contributed words to Wisconsin English, though not as many, since there was not, in simple terms, as large a mass of people to interact with and carry the word usage to their "English" neighbors. Dutch could have played a role in *headcheese* 'meat of the head (and sometimes of feet and inner organs) usually of a pig, boiled, chopped and shaped as a cheese or made into a sausage' (Dutch *hoofdkaas*); *dummkopf* with its Dutch form *domkop*; and *pannicake* (Dutch *pannekoek*, Norwegian *pannekake*). *Opa* is a Dutch as well as a German word. The Dutch probably brought the celebration of a local fair or festival held in the fall by a local church to east central Wisconsin, where the Dutch settled, though there were also Germans and Belgians in the area; the three terms for the festival celebrated by all three groups undoubtedly reinforced each other (Dutch *kermis*, Belgian *kermesse*, and German *Kirmes*). Those of Swiss ancestry in south central Wisconsin also celebrate a similar festival (*kilby*). There these Swiss Americans might have played *hornet*, an outdoor game also played back home in Switzerland.

Still on the topic of food, of Czech origin is *kolacky*, a pastry of pie dough or sweet yeast dough with a sweet topping or filling. The Belgians brought their cabbage sausage *trippe* (pronounced like *trip*) to the lower area of the Green Bay. Many people consider *booyah*, a stew made in a large kettle or drum and frequently served at church picnics in Green Bay and the Fox River Valley, to be of Belgian origin, but other influences might also play a role here. *Majokka* 'a beef stew' is of Finnish origin. Another term brought by the Finns in northern Wisconsin is *sisu*, which is explained on a sign outside Hurley, Wisconsin, at Little Finland, as "the Finnish character of strength and perseverance." The Finnish terms are known and used mostly in northern Wisconsin, where the Finns originally settled, especially in Douglas, Bayfield, Ashland, and Florence counties. The Belgian terms are known mostly around the lower Green Bay, in Kewaunee, Oconto, Brown, and lower Door counties.

More recent immigrant groups such as the Hmong have not yet added commonly used terms to Wisconsin English, but they probably will, following the pattern of earlier immigrant groups. Hispanic immigrants to Wisconsin are relatively few in number compared to some other states; the terms taken into English tend to be used more throughout large sections of the United States or in states with the highest number of Hispanics, especially southwestern states.

You Know These Are Wisconsin Terms

A few iconic terms should be included in any discussion of Wisconsin words. The first that always comes to mind is *bubbler*. Almost everyone lists this first when asked something like "What words do you consider the most 'Wisconsin' of all words?" The term seems to have originated with the Kohler Company near the end of the nineteenth century.[7] To see an original bubbler, visit the state capitol grounds in Madison or look at the picture on Wikipedia's Bubbler entry: this is an original bubbler—the water comes straight up then bubbles back down over itself rather than flows in an arc (see fig. 5.4). As to its use, in this country, it is mostly a Wisconsin term, but it is also used in Rhode Island and part of Massachusetts; the Harvard Dialect Survey of 2002–3 produced a map of its distribution.[8] Note that the map indicates that the term is most widely used in the southern and eastern parts of Wisconsin. (Kohler is in eastern Wisconsin.) While most people in Wisconsin claim *bubbler* as *the* Wisconsin term, it is not really used by everyone throughout the state.

FIGURE 5.4.
Original bubbler at
the Capitol building
in Madison, 2012

Another matter that causes arguments within the state is whether that carbonated sweet beverage should be called *pop* or *soda*. You are correct if you maintain that people in Wisconsin say *soda*, but you are also correct if you maintain that they say *pop*. The pop vs. soda webpage shows this quite clearly: *soda* is used in the eastern part of the state, while *pop* is used in the western half.[9]

Wisconsinites refer to themselves as "cheeseheads" and are proud of it. This was originally a derogatory term flung at us at a sports event by Chicagoans, it is said, but we turned the tables and made it our own. A variant of this word is *cheddarheads*. Other meanings of *cheesehead* are a Green Bay Packers fan and a triangular-shaped piece of foam in the form of a wedge of holey (not holy, in spite of what some Packers fans may think of the team) Swiss (Emmentaler) cheese that can be worn as headgear. You can watch a video clip of the Wisconsin State Assembly honoring the maker of the cheesehead "hat" on March 6, 2012, on YouTube.[10]

If you are looking for somewhere to park your car, you may be able to park it on the street. If not, look for a *parking ramp*, or *ramp*. Near the University of Wisconsin in Madison there is the State St.-Campus Ramp. Around the Square are Capitol ramps. This usage is very common in Madison and can also be found in other larger cities in Wisconsin (see fig. 5.5).

Manitowoc has a tip on its information page that provides a definition of the word *parking lot*: A parking lot is "designed specifically for automobile parking. Alternately called parking structure, parking ramp, parkade or parking deck, it is a facility with a number of floors or levels on which parking takes place." The page goes on to note that "Parking Garage in Manitowoc, however, refers only to an indoor, often underground structure. A garage often requires mechanical ventilation or sprinklers."[11]

You Might Not Know
These Are Wisconsin Terms

Here are a few terms you may know, but that you may not realize the whole country doesn't know. One that surprises a lot of people is *come with* (discussed in the introduction). If you ask people from other areas "Do you want to come with?" they might well wait for you to finish the sentence: "With you? With them? What?" This construction is perfectly good grammar in many Germanic languages—German ("Kommst du mit?"), Dutch, Norwegian, Swedish, Danish, Yiddish, among others. English usually regards the *with* as a preposition which needs an object, but in most of these languages it may be considered an adverb or as in German, as part of a separable verb, which, as the name implies, allows part (*mit* 'with') of the verb (*mitkommen*) to be separated from the rest.

Jerry Apps, in his novel *In a Pickle: A Family Farm Story*, gives us an example of cucumbers being called *pickles*: "Blossoms all over the place

FIGURE 5.5. Parking ramp sign near UW–Madison campus, 2012

and a few little pickles peekin' out here and there" (2007, 22). Where do the pickles grow? "Just about every farmer in this part of Ames County [a mythical county], Wisconsin, had a cucumber patch, called a pickle patch" (2007, 5). One kind of pickle made from ripe cucumbers, or sometimes from watermelon, is a *slippery jim.*

When you were growing up, did you play a game called "Captain may I?" It didn't matter if you were male or female. Or did you call it "Mother may I?" Both terms are used, but *Captain may I?* seems to be a Wisconsin term for the game.

You hunters or fishermen probably know the term *to shine,* which refers to attracting or locating a fish or game animal at night by shining a bright light into their eyes, temporarily immobilizing them, or hunting in such a way. One can shine deer, shine their eyes, or just shine (although one shouldn't). This is also frequently used in Michigan and Minnesota, and less so elsewhere.

Only in Wisconsin?

There do seem to be a few words for which *DARE* has only or almost only evidence of usage from Wisconsin. These include terms such as *court whist* 'a card game', *fire snake* 'a red-bellied snake', *rock rattlesnake* 'a timber rattlesnake', *lannon stone* 'limestone originally quarried in Lannon, Wisconsin', and the following.

In the Ozarks people may *noodle* fish (catch them with their bare hands), but in Wisconsin people used to *noodle* geese: force-feed geese to increase liver size (think foie gras) or body weight (paid for the goose by the pound). This is also from German. The noodles were made of wheat, corn, and/or barley. To my knowledge, this is no longer done.

Chiefly in German settlement areas, including Wisconsin, *ainna* (or *aina* or *enna*) is used as a tag question. A contraction of *ain't it,* and only one of many tag questions such as *isn't it, aren't they, don't you agree?,* this one is used mainly in southeastern Wisconsin, especially in Milwaukee, according to *DARE's* evidence, and not as frequently as in earlier times. Another tag question, *inso,* a contraction of *isn't it so,* has evidence only from southeastern Wisconsin, inso? To hear use of the tag *er no*, listen to Rob Brackenridge on the Wisconsin Englishes website.[12]

An expression that seems strange to me is *start with me last*. The most common use seems to be in restaurants. I first heard it in Fish Creek in 2007 when talking with a server, who was from Kewaunee. She said it's fairly commonly known in the business; other people I have asked have confirmed this. It basically means that you, the patron or customer, are not ready to order when asked by the waitress or waiter, that s/he should take the orders of the others in your party before taking yours. On "The Border: An Eagles Message Board," in a list of Wisconsin expressions, *Start wit* [*sic*] *me last* is defined as "to forfeit one's turn." The example given is "I dunno how to play Sheepshead so good, so start with me last."[13] So it goes beyond restaurants.

AND MORE

You might not know these terms, but you've seen the objects. What do people think of when they think of Milwaukee? Beer, probably. Indeed, our culture is inseparable from our language. And what may come from drinking all that beer? Some people, and not just ones from Wisconsin, may call the oversized stomach a *Milwaukee goiter* or a *German goiter*. A term used in Wisconsin for this, or for the person who has one, is *tavern belly*.

No mention has been made in this chapter of pronunciation (see the preface and elsewhere), but allow me one more remembrance of my first days in Wisconsin: I was amazed to hear that the word *sorry* rhymed with *glory*. And while I immediately (consciously) made *come with* a part of my language, and even though, after having spent more than two-thirds of my life in Wisconsin, I consider myself a Wisconsinite, you will not hear me saying *sorry* with the vowel of *sore*, /sori/.

In some ways, I have an advantage over native Wisconsinites in being able to notice what is unique to Wisconsin, since I didn't grow up with terms like *bakery*, as my daughter Erika did. Although most of the groups of immigrants who settled in Wisconsin and their descendants no longer use the language they brought with them from their country of origin, as discussed in chapter 3, these groups have influenced the

English language spoken in Wisconsin, leaving traces of their origins and history, their culture, in the words we still use today. But our language is always changing; we are constantly deleting words we don't need and adding new terms, from many sources. The terms mentioned here are but a sampling of how Wisconsin English is unique.

NOTES

1. Five volumes of text for the *Dictionary of American Regional English* (*DARE*), through the letter Z, are published. A sixth, supplementary volume appeared in 2012 with maps showing the various words for the same concept throughout the country, e.g., for the sweet carbonated beverage, such terms as *soda, pop, soda pop, soda water, tonic, dope, cold drink,* and *coke* (yes, these all have the same meaning, and yes, *coke* is now used in parts of the country as a generic term, and such use is spreading). It also contained *all* the responses to over four hundred questions from *DARE*'s questionnaire of more than sixteen hundred questions; interviewing was carried out from 1965 to 1970, in every state in the union. For an explanation of the *DARE* maps, see http://dare.wisc .edu/?q=node/17. An electronic version of *DARE* is scheduled for 2013. I draw on information in *DARE* for my discussion of many of the words I mention here, but I go beyond what *DARE* contains.

2. See Wisconsin Historical Society, "State and County Trunk Highway System," http://www.wisconsinhistory.org/archstories/late_roads/sth_cth_sys tem.asp.

3. Words used throughout the United States are not discussed in this chapter. Focus is on words used in Wisconsin, although, as I have mentioned, words such as *trunk* are used in states beyond Wisconsin but are not known nationally.

4. I recently showed a friend from Germany who was visiting us in Madison a flyer about the Bratfest held here every year on Memorial and Labor Day weekends and asked her what that was. She replied that it must be some kind of party where you grill outside. She did not know the term *brat* to refer to a sausage.

5. There is also a Yahoo group that calls itself "Wandering Sheep—For Sheepshead players not in Wisconsin." Description: "Who ever said Wisconsin gets to have all of the Sheepshead fun? Come help me organize clubs and tourneys for those of us lucky enough to enjoy the game . . . but not lucky enough to be a cheesehead. (Cheeseheads are always welcome too)" (http://games .groups.yahoo.com/group/wanderingsheep).

6. *Bismarck* itself is an interesting term. While it appears to be German— and indirectly it is—this name for a jelly doughnut does not exist in Germany.

The name has been traced back to the Hotel Bismarck in Chicago (named for Otto von Bismarck, first chancellor of the German Empire, from 1871 to 1890), which opened in 1894. It is said to have had its own bakery, where it produced fine pastries, including bismarcks.

7. The Wikipedia entry for *bubbler* states that "the Bubbler was developed in 1889 by the then-small Kohler Water Works (now Kohler Company) in Kohler, Wisconsin, which was already well known for its faucet production," although it does not cite a source for this claim (http://en.wikipedia.org/wiki/Bubbler).

8. See http://csumc.wisc.edu/wep/map.htm.

9. See http://popvssoda.com/countystats/total-county.html.

10. See http://www.youtube.com/watch?v=ZAFsB20FmBo.

11. See http://www.yellowpagesgoesgreen.org/Manitowoc-WI/Parking+Lots++Stations++-and-+Garages.

12. See http://csumc.wisc.edu/wep/podcasts/WEP_006.mp3.

13. See http://www.eaglesonlinecentral.com/forum/showthread.php?t=1955&page=5.

CHAPTER 6

Standard English
What Is It? And What Is It Good For?

ERIC RAIMY

S tandard English is fascinating in part because it is mythical. People have a hard time describing exactly what Standard English is, although everyone can identify when it is being used and especially when it is not. And we all agree that it exists. In this chapter I'll walk through who speaks Standard English, what Standard English is and is not, and the role that Standard English should play in our schools. We'll conclude that Standard English can be a useful tool if we understand the role that it plays in our society.

WHO SPEAKS STANDARD ENGLISH?

Let's first set aside the idea that a given English-speaking country is home to Standard English and just assume that there's a Standard English in the United States as opposed to in England (or Canada, Australia, India, Singapore or some other place where children grow up learning English from birth). The reason for setting aside this idea is to make it clear that individual communities decide who speaks Standard English and who doesn't; this can be seen when we consider that if this chapter was being written for British English speakers, Standard English would likely be assumed to be based in London. This is a key point to understand about Standard English: individual speech communities decide who speaks Standard English and who doesn't.

There is, in fact, great variability in judgments about who speaks Standard English, as shown by Dennis Preston's work. Perceptual dialectology is the study of what nonlinguists think about regional differences in language. Preston asks different communities of speakers questions about language and then analyzes their answers. (Note that this work is simply about attitudes and perceptions of speech in particular regions; it doesn't involve data, like samples of speech or examples of regional features.) Figures 6.1, 6.2, and 6.3 present the results of some of Preston's work. The first figure asks people to rate the "correctness" of English spoken in each of the fifty states. The rating system is that 10 is "most correct" while 1 is "least correct." The numbers for the states are the average from the group. The averages happen to be no lower than 3 or higher than 9, which explains why the scale only represents ratings between these numbers. These figures also present the ratings in a graphic way; enlarged darker states indicate a higher rating while shrunken lighter states have a lower rating. Figure 6.1 presents the results from respondents from southeastern Michigan asked to rate the "correctness" of the English spoken in different states.

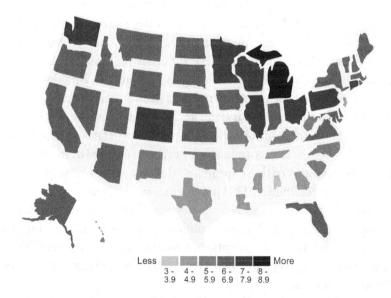

FIGURE 6.1. Correctness: the view from Michigan (Adapted from Preston 1998)

In figure 6.1, Michiganders consider the most "correct" English to be spoken in Michigan (the darkest state in the map) and then slightly less correct English in Washington, Colorado, Minnesota, Wisconsin, Illinois, Ohio, Pennsylvania, and Massachusetts. The least "correct" English is spoken in Alabama (the smallest and lightest shaded state), with Texas, Arkansas, Louisiana, Mississippi, Tennessee, Georgia, and New Jersey a little more "correct." The remaining states are somewhere in the middle.

A reasonable way to interpret the Michigan perspective is as suggesting that "midwesterners" speak the most correct English and that as one moves away from the Midwest and especially as one moves further south, speakers use less correct English. This interpretation seems to be borne out by the map; there are only a few wrinkles, such as Florida being ranked higher than it should based on its southernness (maybe the "snowbirds" raise its score) and New Jersey being ranked lower based on its proximity to the northeast. And this interpretation also matches many intuitions about who speaks the most "correct" English in the United States. But we'll see that common sense does not always serve us well when it comes to understanding language.

Figure 6.2 is based on responses from college-aged subjects in Alabama answering the same question the Michiganders did. We can immediately see that Alabamians have different opinions about where "correct" English is spoken. According to Alabamians, Michigan is no longer the home of the most "correct" English. Instead, the most "correct" English is spoken in Maryland and Delaware (the darkest states), followed by a patchwork of other "more correct" states as one heads westward. There is no centralization of "correct" English in the Midwest in the opinions of these speakers. Alabama is no longer the home of the least correct English. That judgment is instead reserved for Texas, Louisiana, Mississippi, and New Jersey (the lightest shaded states in the map) in a tiebreaker. It is more difficult to create a narrative for this pattern of correctness judgments, but we will try in a moment. First, consider figure 6.3, which shows the results from asking Alabamians a different question.

Figure 6.3 is based on the Alabama subjects rating the states on how "pleasant" the English is. The pattern is similar to the pattern for

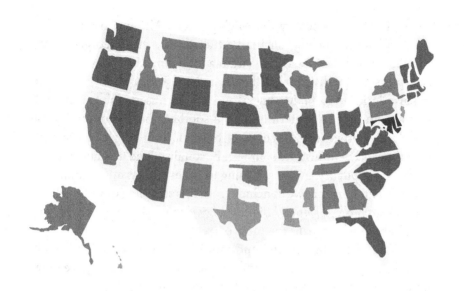

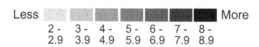

Less 2- 3- 4- 5- 6- 7- 8- More
2.9 3.9 4.9 5.9 6.9 7.9 8.9

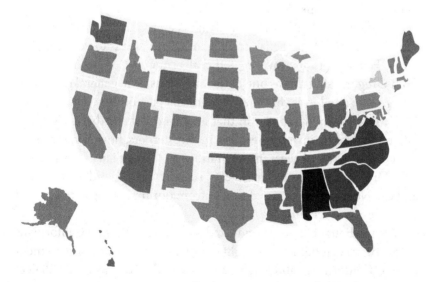

FIGURES 6.2–6.3. Correctness (*top*) and pleasantness (*bottom*): the view from Alabama (Adapted from Preston 1998)

"correctness" produced by the Michiganders. Alabama has the most "pleasant"-sounding English (darkest shading), with Georgia, South Carolina, North Carolina, and Virginia following closely behind. The least pleasant English can be heard in New Jersey, then New York, and also in Minnesota, Michigan, and Massachusetts (shrunken with light shading). This pattern follows a southern-based commonsense view that southerners' language is pleasant sounding because they are polite and demonstrate southern hospitality. The northerners lack southern hospitality and so are going to be less "pleasant"-sounding.

The main thing that we conclude from this sampling of Dennis Preston's research on perceptual dialectology is that there is no single consensus about who speaks the most correct or most pleasant English in the United States. In fact, an important issue is whether, when people answer the question who uses the most correct English, they are judging language or are expressing other judgments about the groups of people. Maybe "correctness" is a placeholder for education level or a placeholder for cultural similarity. Stepping back and thinking about the basis for our judgments about other people's language is important for understanding what Standard English is and is not. I return to this question later in this chapter.

A more neutral question about language judgments would be how similar you think the English spoken in a given area is to your English. Laura Hartley (1999) investigated dialect perception among people from Oregon using this as one of the questions. The general result that we are interested in is that they recognize a part of the country as the "Midwest," place Wisconsin in that area, and believe that they speak differently from midwesterners. We midwesterners, however, earn similar correctness and pleasantness ratings to Oregonians for the most part. Oregonians view other dialects, such as those found in the South and the Northeast, as more different from our midwestern dialect and also as less correct and pleasant.

Carmen Fought (2002) conducted a similar study using Californians as the source of judgments. Fought found there wasn't strong agreement among Californians about where one would find a Midwest dialect or whether Wisconsin counted as Midwest for this purpose. Judgment about the quality of midwestern speech was also mixed; some respondents thought that midwesterners did not have an accent and some thought that they had a pronounced accent. The combination of Fought and Hartley's work suggests that a national opinion is developing about Midwest speech.

To consider what we Wisconsinites think about ourselves, we can look to Erica Benson, from the University of Wisconsin–Eau Claire. Benson runs the Wisconsin Folk Linguistics Project, which conducts research about Wisconsinites' attitude about and sensitivity to language variation in Wisconsin. Benson has asked residents of Eau Claire this question about other parts of Wisconsin. Figure 6.4 presents judgments of subjects from Eau Claire as to how similar the English spoken in different locations in Wisconsin is to the English spoken in Eau Claire, with the scale being from 1 (the same) to 4 (different).

According to the judgments represented in figure 6.4, the English in Milwaukee is the most different from that of Eau Claire while La Crosse's is the most similar. Long-form responses from a number of the subjects provide some context for the basis of these judgments. Some themes in the long-form responses are that because the southern part of the state is closer to Illinois, speakers from Madison and Milwaukee sound like they are from there and that northern Wisconsin speakers (Rhinelander in the map) sound different because of proximity to Canada. Another way to look at this is as suggesting there is a common stereotype about "up nort" that provides the basis for thinking of Rhinelander as different from Eau Claire. Milwaukee is the one true urban area in the state, so its English must also be different according to common sense. Madison is not as urban as Milwaukee but is regarded as distinctive within the state owing to its progressive and liberal politics, suggesting that it too should be different from Eau Claire.

The additional comments collected in the Wisconsin Folk Linguistics Project help us understand the commonalities between Benson's and Preston's work. Research such as theirs that tracks people's judgment about how other people speak English provides ample evidence that we are sensitive to differences in how people talk. Furthermore, this sensitivity is somehow connected to our beliefs about what kinds of English are spoken by what groups of people in what geographic locations. Note that most of these judgments are not based on actual

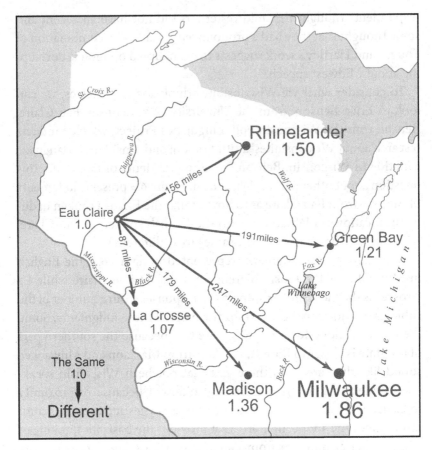

FIGURE 6.4. Perceived similarity of English spoken in other communities to Eau Claire (Adapted from map created by Erica Benson, University of Wisconsin–Eau Claire, for the Wisconsin Folk Linguistics Project. A factor of one suggests similarity; a factor of four indicates difference.)

accurate real-world knowledge, meaning that we can have these opinions regardless of whether we know anyone from such-and-such a location or any grammatical details about such-and such a dialect. To put this another way, judgments about language that are collected as part of folk linguistics or perceptual dialectology are all subjective and based on local beliefs. This is one of the most interesting aspects of language behavior in humans. We all believe that there is such a thing as good and bad language, but it is impossible to find an objective answer as to what is good or bad. We may not be fully aware of the fact that there is no objective answer until someone tells us about it. In the next section, we explore some of the reasons behind our agreement that there is a correct or Standard English out there but disagreement about who speaks it.

What Is Standard English?

To begin to understand what Standard English is we must first distinguish between nonstandard and ungrammatical. Linguists reserve the term *ungrammatical* for words or phrases that are impossible for a given language. *Nonstandard* words or phrases on the other hand are possible but are not socially valued (I clarify this in a moment). To understand the distinction between nonstandard and ungrammatical let's consider the following list of sentences. Each sentence is meant to express the same idea. The first sentence is standard, but from there each sentence becomes less standard in some way. At some point, the sentence passes over into the ungrammatical, but note that there is no straight path from standard to ungrammatical in these examples.

(1) a. The hunters did not shoot the small deer.
　　b. Them hunters didn't shoot them small deer.
　　c. Them hunters didn't shoot no small deers.
　　d. Dem hunters didn't shoot no small deers.
　　e. *Hunters dem didn't shoot no deers small.
　　f. *Hunters the didn't shoot the deer small.

Sentence (1a) is a completely "standard" sentence of English. (1b) replaces both instances of *the* with *them*. This is a common dialect feature in North American English and is nonstandard but not ungrammatical. (1c) replaces the second *them* with *no*, producing "negative concord," or a double negative. Again, we can find many dialectal examples of double negation in English over the past four hundred years. As noted in the introduction, Shakespeare himself used and wrote double negatives, which is not ungrammatical for English. In

(1d) we see the nonstandard phonological replacement of the *th* sound of the beginning of the word *them* with a *d* sound. This phonological substitution, along with other ways of eliminating the *th* sounds, is extremely common in many kinds of English, and while definitely nonstandard it is not ungrammatical. This example also features the word *deer* marked with the plural *s*. For many speakers of English, *deer* can be pluralized in this fashion, but it is nonstandard.

Sentences (1e) and (1f) are ungrammatical examples (linguists place an asterisk * before a sentence to indicate that it is ungrammatical). We turn (1d) into the ungrammatical rather than simply nonstandard (1e) by moving a few words around. We have, for example, moved *dem* from in front of *hunters* to after it. This change means that the determiner (words like *the, an, a,* and phonological equivalents like *de,* etc.) now comes after the noun (*hunter* in this example), which is impossible in English. In fact, this is ungrammatical for English broadly speaking: no person who grows up from childhood speaking English ever speaks in this manner. However, such determiner placement is more or less possible in Norwegian. Another change in this example is that we have moved the adjective *small* from before *deers* to after it. The placement of an adjective after the noun it modifies is impossible in English but is possible in languages like French or Spanish. (1f) is the same as (1e) except for fixing the phonological nonstandardness; this example is meant to show that pronunciation can be perfect but the phrase can still be ungrammatical.

Having considered the difference between nonstandard and ungrammatical, we can begin to delve into the difference between standard and nonstandard English. Walt Wolfram and Natalie Shilling-Estes's book *American English* posits three basic types of English: formal standard, informal standard, and vernacular. These categories go beyond standard versus nonstandard, but their utility is immediately apparent.

Formal Standard English is written and is also the most formal spoken language. A formal standard is identified by specific rules that are prescribed from authoritative sources such as the educational system, dictionaries, and grammars. If there is a question about whether a form is standard or not, these sources provide a definitive yes-or-no answer. Because of the connection between language authorities and a formal standard, only people who have full access to the educational system have a chance to learn this variety of English. Having full access in this context usually means being able to attend college (see the next section). A final crucial feature of any formal standard version of a language is that it considers any change (even natural ones) from the prescribed forms to be incorrect and detrimental to the language.

We now turn to informal Standard English, which is based on spoken language and not writing. This variety is defined by how people actually talk and has many different acceptable forms based on location and situation. The details (words, pronunciations, word order patterns, etc.) are determined locally by speakers both through their speech behavior and their judgments about their speech behavior. Everyone learns a form of the informal standard. We do not need to go to school to learn this variety of English because everyone will learn the informal standard of whatever speech community they grow up in. It's the language variety that we all use when we are relaxed and being ourselves.

Finally, vernacular English is similar to informal Standard English in that it is based on spoken language. Vernacular English is defined by how people speak and by the judgments members of the speech community make about this speech. The difference between vernacular English and informal Standard English is that the vernacular is defined in a negative way as having particular unwanted features. Swearing, double negatives, and saying *axe* for *ask* are some clear examples of common vernacular English features. Remember that the vernacular is defined locally so other common variations in English such as *warsh* for *wash, fixin' to*, and double modals in such constructions as *I might could do that* may or may not be vernacular depending on the time and place. Everyone learns some form of vernacular English even if they never use it themselves (for example, some people never use swear words, but everyone knows what they are), just as everyone learns informal Standard English.

Schools and What to Do with Standard English

When we put these three varieties of English together we can understand much about what "standard" or "correct" English is and is not.

The most important point is the interaction between the natural way we learn language and how we learn language in schools. Everyone learns the local vernacular form of language first, and this is the language that kids come to school with. All children arrive with a different form of the informal standard that they have learned from the community they are being raised in. This community is the child's family, play group, day-care center or preschool, and so forth. The formal standard is taught in schools and is normally *only* learned in schools. Thus, children who spend more time in school and have a more positive experience there will be more successful at learning formal Standard English. The most successful in learning formal Standard English will be the people who complete a college education.

Because of the close relationship between education and formal Standard English, one way the term "Standard English" is used is as a proxy for "educated." This state of affairs provides an explanation as to how it happens that everyone agrees there is something called "Standard English" but how few people actually speak it, if anybody does. Formal Standard English only really exists in written form. For spoken language, it is informal Standard English that counts as "Standard English." The rules of this version of English are locally defined, so there is inevitably a mismatch between the spoken version of Standard English and written Standard English. The fact that the written form is not the same as the spoken form is the likely source of both our difficulty in defining Standard English and any sort of linguistic self-loathing that we may feel. It is common for a person to be insecure about how they speak, especially if they don't reside in the speech community that they grew up in.

The dual nature of Standard English allows us to think about the opinions that a speech community has about a speaker based on the speaker's speech behaviors. We want our professionals to be educated, and thus we expect them to use Standard English. We generally think people who use Standard English to be educated and competent. We expect professionals like lawyers to be able to write clearly and to not make spelling mistakes. In spoken language, we expect them to follow the prescriptive rules laid down for writing and to use "bigger," less common words. Naturally, these expectations do not give any indication about their professional abilities, but if they fail to fulfill the expectations, people may doubt their competence.

However, one cannot assume a speaker is less competent because they do not use Standard English, whether in written or spoken form. People in jobs that do not expressly require formal education may be able to use a more natural informal standard (or even the vernacular) without being judged, so that master carpenters can sound "less educated" without having their competence at their craft called into question. Again, no conclusions can be drawn about how smart these people are based on what kind of English they speak. Each skilled labor, whether it is white, pink, or blue collar, has its own specialized knowledge. College provides access to the store of information that is required for white-collar work, while technical schools and apprenticeships provide access to the knowledge required to excel in skilled blue-collar jobs. Each has its own language style, and this explains why we can often pick out mismatches (a college-educated person working in a blue-collar job or a non-college-educated person working in a white-collar job). Again, a person's use of formal Standard English only indicates that they have gone through much if not all of our formal education system but does not indicate anything about their raw intelligence, wisdom, moral character, or how much they know.

Because formal Standard English is so tied to formal education, we should think about how different varieties of language like formal standards, informal standards, and vernaculars are treated in schools. Are we educating our children about language variation and how different language varieties play out in society? A first step is to ask ourselves what role we want our educational system to play in shaping our future. If we think that Standard English matters in our society, then we may want to have our educational system teach our children about it. Currently, students are typically not educated about what Standard English is and what role it plays in our society. The result of this is that the average American harbors both positive and negative prejudices about language use. A person who uses the vernacular or informal standard may be judged as being uneducated or "incorrect," a negative prejudice, while a person who uses the standard formal may be judged as being smart and "correct," a positive prejudice. A rough nonlinguistic equivalent of this type of prejudice is that if a person is not wearing a tie then they can't be educated or give you good advice, while any person who does wear a tie is automatically educated and correct about everything. A geographically based variant of this kind of prejudice is that if the person is from Wisconsin, then you can trust them in all things, while if the person is not from Wisconsin, then you can't trust them one bit. These examples are overstated and oversimplified but unfortunately are not entirely off the mark when language is concerned.

An alternative approach in teaching Standard English to our children is to incorporate more explicit information about different varieties of language. If we begin teaching our children about different types of language and how they are used, then it is possible that our prejudices based on language will be reduced. The educational system, especially equal access to the educational system, has an important role here because children start out in school already knowing a lot about language. They already know about "good language" (*please* and *thank you*) and "bad language" (swearing, saying *hate*, etc.), which is different among different groups of people owing to dialects and accents, and they have opinion as to what counts as good and bad language. Schools can be a place where these differences can be used as material to learn not only about how language works but also about critical thinking and other cultures. A key aspect to this idea is to take a descriptive and comparative approach to language study. The descriptive part of this approach requires working with how people actually talk, which will allow kids to study the informal standard varieties that exist in their classroom. The comparative part entails noticing and talking about the differences in the informal standards that exist in the classroom, school, or community. A very interesting thing happens when students are taught explicitly about different informal standards and the formal standard: students end up speaking vernacular English less and thus using language that is closer to the formal standard. Teaching kids to use a language variety that is closer to the formal standard is one of the goals of our educational system.

Improving the effectiveness of our educational system in teaching formal Standard English is a goal that everyone should be able to agree on. There are additional benefits beyond the mastery of formal standard

English to the suggestions mentioned here being adopted. One potential benefit from the comparative method is that students will match their language behaviors properly to different types of language expectations. Using texting (an informal standard) abbreviations in an essay for an English class is bad form, just as using proper punctuation and spelling out every word is bad form in a text. Explicitly knowing the differences among different styles of language such as texting, e-mail, literary essays, scientific reports, memos, journalistic reporting, and so forth only enriches and improves a student's language abilities. Another potential benefit is that there may be less prejudice toward others in general if we recognize that many of our language prejudices are unfounded. There's nothing to conclude about a person who uses the phrase *fixin' to*, drops their *gs*, uses the habitual *be* (discussed in chapter 7), or ends their sentence with *you betcha!* other than that the person is either from a place near where you grew up or not or from a similar social group or not. The more you know about the details of language, the better you can effectively speak, read, write, and interpret what you hear and read.

Conclusion

This chapter has introduced the notion of Standard English and attitudes about it. One main point is that most folks hold unquestioned attitudes about varieties of English, especially those that differ from their own. Another main point is that the judgments speakers make about varieties of English can be used in our educational system as a teaching resource for improving the teaching of Standard English. By analyzing differences in language varieties currently used by children in all school systems, we can improve understanding of how Standard English works, increase use of Standard English, and possibly decrease prejudice against speakers of nonstandard varieties of English.

Suggestions for Further Reading

Below is a list of topics raised in this chapter and starting points to read more about them if you are interested. The full references are at the end of the book.

Comparative method in teaching: Rickford 1999

Double negatives in Shakespeare: Parker and Riley 2010

Education and power: Chomsky 2003

Perceptual dialectology: Erica Benson, Wisconsin Folk Linguistics Project; Fought 2002; Hartley 1999; Preston 1998

Standard English: Biber, Johansson, Leech, Conrad, and Finegan 1999; Huddleston and Pullum 2005; Wolfram and Shilling-Estes 2006

CHAPTER 7

Ethnicity and Language

THOMAS PURNELL

Ethnicity is a major theme of this book: the fact that speakers use the language of the speech community they grew up in, speech communities that emerged from Native American, Yankee, or immigrant communities, is what makes Wisconsin Englishes a perpetual topic of lively casual and academic discussions around the state. These three ethnically affiliated groups are covered in other chapters, although we should recognize that in all areas the theme of ethnicity looms large. This chapter aims to clarify the often socially problematic place of a fourth ethnically affiliated speech community, the African American speech community, in Wisconsin language matters. In a community of speakers representing, at the national level, the most stigmatized variety of American English, language entangles with history, politics, education, housing, jobs, laws, and discrimination in many ways. Race does matter, especially in language—but perhaps not in ways of which the public is aware. The goal of this chapter is not to give each nuance of race and language the depth and gravity the topic demands; instead, the aim here is to enable all of us to have a coherent discussion of race, cutting through language we consider, following Manning Nash and others, to be a surface pointer of more important issues.

In *The Cauldron of Ethnicity in the Modern World* (1989), Nash argues that social groups are defined by boundaries that are perceived only through superficial, surface pointers. These pointers include such

97

cultural objects as dress and language. We often, then, dress and speak like people we consider relatives, people with whom we share a meal or drink, and people who share our beliefs. This plays itself out in Wisconsin, community by community, especially where some defining characteristic is particularly strong. For example, German heritage runs through much of Sheboygan. It is such a strong feature of the community, in fact, that residents who are of Irish heritage from Sheboygan have admitted to being mistaken as German on account of the way they speak. In a similar vein, African Americans in the Milwaukee suburbs (e.g., Wauwatosa, Hartland, etc.), which are predominantly white, may sound "white." This pattern arises because people living in mid- or small-size locales are going to similar schools, engaging civically with each other, and so on. In larger locations, the groups divide the community. For example, Milwaukee is segregated, and this segregation reinforces the boundaries leading to distinct speech patterns between blacks and whites. With this general framework in mind, we now turn to a consideration of what language variety is associated with African Americans in Wisconsin.

What African American English Is and Is Not

African American English is a term identifying a speech variety used by speakers—black, white, Hispanic, Italian, whatever—growing up in a geographic area that is predominately African American. Traditionally, Americans in general associate the most vernacular, that is, the most nonwhite, variety of English as being African American English. Just as some individuals with German heritage have a strong accent, while other speakers of English identifying strongly with a Teutonic heritage that lacks any hint of the motherland, so too African Americans span a range from Standard American English speakers to a nonstandard variety labeled "ebonics," "black English," "African American vernacular English" (AAVE), "black street speech" (John Baugh's phrase), "jive," "slang," and so forth (Lisa Green, in her authoritative text on the subject, lists no less than fifteen different terms for the speech variety.) Each of these common terms has a history and focuses on a particular dynamic. In 1973, Robert Williams and other black academics coined the term *ebonics* (*ebony* plus *phonics*, or, approximately, *black sounds*) as a means of reclaiming the African heritage of the speech forms. The historical narrative of the term—as told by both Robert Williams and Ernie Smith—is worth reading, and it can be contextualized as a way of taking a frontal approach to pervasive linguistic profiling and discrimination of African Americans. This approach is essentially one of language planning, that is, of making a conscious change to language based on public policy. Unfortunately, as Baugh points out in *Beyond Ebonics*, the term has gained, in large part due to public backlash to the Oakland School Board's linking the term with failed educational policy in 1997, some degree of culturally negative and perhaps in the worst case comical associations. AAVE focuses on the differentness of the variety from mainstream white varieties while joining it to other varieties of Englishes spoken in the United States of America. Black street speech addresses the urban variety arising primarily from the emancipation-Reconstruction-great migration progression that ended with a large number of African Americans taking up residence in urban areas, particularly outside of the rural South, to escape segregation and secure stable employment in factories. This very cursory unpacking of some of the more common terms affiliated with this speech community should be bookended by noting that when Salikoko Mufwene of the University of Chicago surveyed university students, they could not agree entirely on an appropriate term.

The variety of speech discussed here is the most widely studied variety of American English. Unsurprisingly, there are many sideboards piled high with books covering each of these terms. Scholarly interest in African American English got under way around the time of Walt Wolfram's 1969 description of a speech community in Detroit in the context of the revolutions in the science of language generally and sociolinguistic variation specifically (driven by Noam Chomsky and William Labov, respectively). The study of African American English is not only a highly valuable academic discipline but also provides us with a way to understand the space in which we all live. Titles published in the field include, but are not limited to, the following works, listed by terms in their title: *Ebonics: The True Language of Black Folks* (Williams 1975) and *Beyond Ebonics: Linguistic Pride and Racial Prejudice* (Baugh

2000); *A Sociolinguistic Description of Detroit Negro Speech* (Wolfram 1969); *Black English: Its History and Usage in the United States* (Dillard 1973), *Talkin and Testifyin: The Language of Black America* (Smitherman 1977), *Black Talk: Words and Phrases from the Hood to the Amen Corner* (Smitherman 1994), *Black Street Speech* (Baugh 1988) and *You Know My Steez: An Ethnographic and Sociolinguistic Study of Styleshifting in a Black American Speech Community* (Alim 2004); *Language in the Inner City: Studies in the Black English Vernacular* (Labov 1973) and *African American Vernacular English: Features, Evolution, Educational Implications* (Rickford 1999); and *Out of the Mouths of Slaves: African American Language and Educational Malpractice* (Baugh 1999) and *African American English* (Green 2002).

Two terms in the list need special attention. The terms *jive* and *slang* are often used to reflect an understanding that words of this variety can be nonstandard (see also the introduction). Technically, these terms deal primarily with words: *jive* is related to jargon or domain-specific words and *slang* to what can be most easily thought of as words with a short shelf life related to, as Michael Adams claims in *Slang*, our need to fit into a specific group. We can quickly (and eagerly) toss these terms aside as characterizations of the entire variety. Many times they reflect a narrow and uninformed idea that fundamentally African American English is simply a set of different words that are fashionable by younger speakers. In fact, African American English is on par as a legitimate system with all other forms of American English precisely because it demonstrates predictable patterns in the sounds of words, the way words are made up, the meanings of words, the manner in which words are arranged in phrases, the manner of talking, group communication events, and so on. The terms *jive* and *slang* are inadequate to reflect the rich array of features found in African American English. Nevertheless, educated and politically strong individuals, even blacks, have used these terms when speaking of the need for younger speakers to use Standard American English to improve their economic prospects. On January 3, 1997, the Linguistic Society of America went so far in its resolution on the Oakland (California) School Board ebonics controversy as to include *slang* in its list of what African American English is not.

By way of illustration of the systematicity of African American English, we can briefly consider the many forms that a verb can take. Standard American English conjugates verbs by time (present, past, and future) and by what linguists call "aspect" (simple, progressive, perfect, perfect progressive). Although there are other nuances involving the modal verbs (*should, could,* and the like), that is the extent of the standard variety. Green (2002) demonstrates a more extensive verbal conjugation pattern for African American English (see table 7.1), using forms of the verbs *to drink* and *to fly.* It should be noted that African Americans have at their disposal the remote and resultant aspects in nonstandard variants in addition to the standard times and aspects.

It used to be claimed that the insular characteristics of the African American speech community arising from long-term segregation and Jim Crow laws led to African American English being fairly uniform compared to white varieties. Recently, however, there have been a number of studies on African American English sound systems

TABLE 7.1. Summary of past marking

Type of past	Marker and verb form	Meaning
Simple past	drunk/flown	Time before the present
Preterit had	had drunk/flown	Time before the present, often used in narrative contexts
Remote past	BIN drunk/flown	Remote past
Past perfect (pluperfect)	had drunk/flown	Past before the past
Remote past perfect	had BIN drunk/flown	Past before the remote past
Resultant state	dən drunk/flown	State of having ended or having been finished, can occur with some states in special contexts

Source: Modified from Green 2002, 93 (28).
Notes: BIN is spelled in upper case letters to indicate the grammatical form as distinct from the standard *been*. The use of *dən* indicates that the vowel in *done* is always the reduced vowel.

demonstrating that local variations are a mix of shared local sounds and features that transcend location (pan–African American features). Milwaukee was one location that showed such variation. Forty years have passed since the end of the great migration, after the Civil War and Reconstruction, when African Americans sought jobs in the north. It would be surprising, then, if younger speakers did not display more local features that would identify them as African Americans from Milwaukee, as opposed to Chicago or Jackson, Mississippi. For example, in the South, many speakers do not pronounce the *r* sound when it follows a vowel in the same syllable, as in *hair* (approximating something like *hay-uh*). In Milwaukee these "r" sounds are more often pronounced.

One study compared speakers from the core northwest side of Milwaukee with either speakers in the peripheral suburbs of Waukesha or Wauwatosa or those who had increased contact with non-AAVE forms through one white parent (Purnell 2009). The degree to which speakers modified their speech patterns was measured by changes in the pronunciation of vowels. Of note, the vowel in the word *bite* is a diphthong, specifically, a vowel that begins with the tongue low, as with the vowel in *bot*, and that ends up more like the vowel in *beet*. White speakers in the Upper Midwest can pronounce the vowel in *bite* (but not so much in *bide* or *buy*) in a more Canadian-like way, that is, starting with a vowel like the *u* in *but*. In the study, African American speakers who had more exposure to white speech forms could change their speech and make accommodations for the white speaker they were talking to. These speakers were more likely to also "raise" their vowel to mimic the white speaker and for some speakers even overcompensate the end gesture of the vowel. Moreover, speakers in Milwaukee, regardless of experience with other speakers or their association with speakers of any ethnic group, produce the vowel in *bide* with a diphthong and not as a single, monophthongal vowel, as in a strongly southern pronunciation, where *bod* and *bide* are near homophones.

CAUSE FOR CONCERN

The narrative of African Americans in Wisconsin follows the same story of other Africans taken forcibly to the New World. Africans and their descendants were made subservient to white slave traders in part by being provided with new clothes, mores, and language varieties. Very long and painful story short, the ensuing southern black-white separation through the Jim Crow years and the great migration to the urban north brought African Americans to Wisconsin very late (McHugh 1987). Figures 7.1 and 7.2 show the distribution of African Americans in 1900 and 2010. The oldest large settlements of African Americans were in factory communities of Beloit and Milwaukee during the period

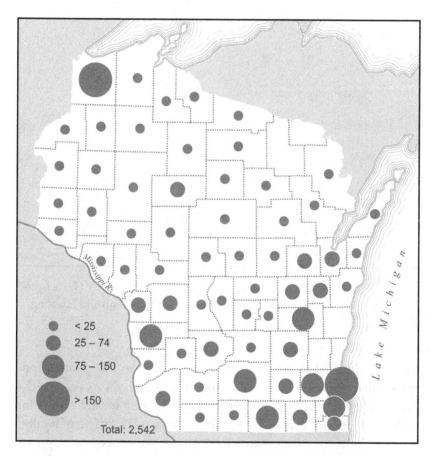

FIGURE 7.1. African American population in 1900, by county (Data from the 1900 U.S. census. The absence of a symbol from a particular county indicates no African Americans were counted there in 1900.)

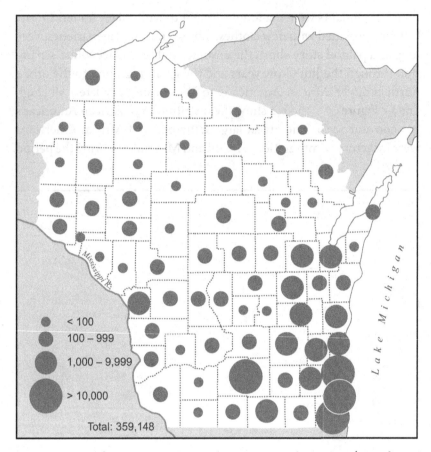

FIGURE 7.2. African American population in 2010, by county (Data from 2010 U.S. census, table DP-1, "Profile of General Population and Housing Characteristics.")

just before World War II. In Milwaukee, home to the greatest concentration of African Americans, it became clear in the 1940s that the Progressive state had a long way to go in actualizing social freedom for African Americans. Eventually, housing compacts legally (here "legally" is not synonymous with reasonable or with the concept of supporting equal rights) squared out a little, tidy section of Milwaukee—W. North, W. Juneau, N. 3rd, and N. 12th streets (Ranney 1995, Trotter 1985)—where landlords were allowed to rent to the migrating African

Americans. This geographic configuration led to one of the most consistently segregated cities, a configuration that has persisted to the present time. In 2008, Reynolds Farley of the University of Michigan's Population Studies Center calculated that in order for there to be the same ratio of blacks and whites in all blocks of the city, 75 percent of blacks would have to move. Maps produced using any year of the census data collected in the city since 1940—for example, see figure 7.3—stunningly demonstrate the effect of the compacts; such maps consistently display a comet-shaped community of African Americans with the tail of the comet flying out to the northwest, pointing toward Fond du Lac.

Housing, employment, and language constitute parts of a troubling social merry-go-round that African Americans in racially segregated locales cannot seem to get off. In the following narrative, it is important to keep one's focus on the centrality of the issue of ethnicity in Wisconsin. One of the goals for this book is to begin discussions of the complexities of this problem: how do we effect lasting change that benefits everyone in our communities across the state, including intercity schools? In 2010, John Pustejovsky of Marquette University arranged for the editors of this volume to talk with a group of students about their linguistic experiences as African American Wisconsinites. The students shared freely. One striking thing about this conversation was that it constituted an open discussion about race through linguistic experiences; we hope that as citizens of the state engage in such discussions they will get past the *jive* and *slang* mischaracterizations of the variety and its speakers.

HOW NATURAL SOUNDING IS RACE?

The narrative of our understanding of African American English in Wisconsin begins with a newly hired professor to Stanford University, John Baugh (Purnell, Idsardi, and Baugh 1999). Baugh, an Ivy League–educated professor of linguistics, was raised in Philadelphia and Los Angeles and developed a knack on the playground for switching between African American English, Standard American English, and Chicano English. The narrative Professor Baugh relates of the events that took

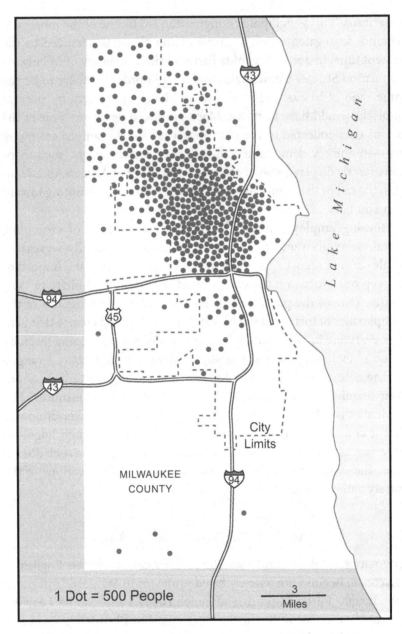

FIGURE 7.3. Distribution of African Americans in Milwaukee County in 2010, by census tract (Data from the 2010 U.S. census, table DP-1, "Profile of General Population and Housing Characteristics")

place when arriving in Palo Alto involves landlords setting up appointments over the phone in Standard American English but shutting the door in his face when they saw he was an African American. The relevant piece of the ensuing academic study was that Baugh called landlords in the San Francisco Bay area who were advertising apartments for rent using the three dialects, leading with the phrase "Hello. I'm calling about the apartment advertised in the paper." The results by community demonstrated that his choice of dialect influenced whether or not he could set up an appointment to see the apartment. To double check that his renditions of the three dialects were perceptually authentic (note that it didn't matter what race he was), Baugh played recordings of samples of him speaking using three dialects—(white) Standard English, African American English, and Chicano English—as well as recordings of other speakers uttering the same sentence to students at Stanford. His renditions were perceived as he intended them, either as being as good as or better than the other voices of monodialectal speakers. The word *hello* alone was then played for mostly white students at the University of Delaware and University of Wisconsin–Madison. In a forced choice experiment, listeners identified the word as being in the intended dialect at a rate well over chance. Given that these samples were a mere half a second long or shorter, this finding suggests that listeners make categorical distinctions almost immediately. In making this research on linguistic profiling public on National Public Radio (Smith 2001) and in an ABC 20/20 segment from 2002, Baugh was at pains to argue that hearing differences by race is not prejudice. During the NPR program, (now retired) appellate judge Richard Knepper voiced the fear of many listeners: "If I say I know what 'black' sounds like, that makes me sound like I'm a racist." We might wonder whether listeners would disavow hearing race because of this. The idea that race blindness applies to what we hear was put to a legal test in Milwaukee. This time, however, the area of discrimination was not housing but employment.

In the fall of 2001, Dennis McBride, a lawyer for the Equal Employment Opportunity Commission (EEOC) in Milwaukee, filed a complaint against the Target Corporation claiming racial discrimination against African American applicants by the management team of the regional office of Target in New Berlin (*EEOC v. Target*). One of the plaintiffs, Kelisha White, was finishing her studies in 2001 at Marquette when she applied for a management position at Target (see page 5 of the opinion) and mailed in her résumé, leaving follow-up messages with the company's management recruiter Matthew Armiger. Time passed and a hunch led her to dumb down her resume and change the name to a recognizably white one (Sarah Brucker). A white friend placed a follow-up call, and her call was returned by the next day.

McBride, for his part, interviewed a number of individuals tied to the case, the plaintiffs and many people from Target. All the interviews were conducted in a similar fashion. He would ask the person whether he or she could perceive different types of voices over the phone, first using the voices of familiar people, then the voices of people from different groups, including those of elderly, male, female, nonlocal, and nonnative speakers. After each one, the interviewee, without exception, answered that there was no problem perceiving a person on the phone as belonging to one of these groups. However, when he asked about the race of an individual, some of the speakers admitted they couldn't tell, while others claimed they could. This split in answers in the interview begs the question of whether people can hear differences, though they may deny that they can hear racial differences even as they admit to hearing all other features of speech communities. District court judge Randa dismissed the case. Consequently, the EEOC appealed the dismissal in the Seventh Circuit Court of Appeals in Chicago. Circuit judge Cudahy's opinion in essence agreed that Arminger could have suspected that individuals leaving messages were African American. Before the case could go to trial in 2007, the Target Corporation admitted to nothing and settled financially with the EEOC and the plaintiffs.

While a judicial decision in this instance never materialized, and this kind of auditory-testing procedure lacked a legal precedent, academics took the matter into their own hands. Bill Idsardi, one of the coauthors of the final report on the Baugh experiments sketched here, and his students at the University of Maryland found that when they played the African American and white *hello* samples for listeners in a brain imaging study, the auditory cortex activated in different, but systematic, patterns (Scharinger, Monahan, and Idsardi 2011). Such neuromagnetic studies as this one provide insight to passive (preattentive) cognitive processes. Idsardi hypothesizes that since the preattentive responses can be found in people who are asleep or in a coma, the differences are getting into the brain and are processed by people regardless of whether the individuals are prone to discrimination or not. This experiment supports Baugh's point that hearing differences is natural and merely a cognitive function. Higher-order cognition, such as the processing of our volition, which occurs after preattentive processing, is when discrimination can come into the picture. We can interpret those denials from McBride's interviewees, then, as being most likely an attempt to avoid (at best) appearing as one who engages in racial discrimination.

CONCLUSION

In this chapter, I have presented some commonly accepted and some relatively new evidence that African American English, the dominant nonstandard, ethnically affiliated variety of American English, is a linguistically relevant variety just as any white variety might be. Moreover, I have tried to show that it is not necessary for listeners to deny that they can "hear race."

So, what does the situation of African Americans in Wisconsin tell us? First, the linguistic structures of African American English continually beg to be recognized as a distinct variety from white speech; being contrastive to white speech implies that the variety constitutes a linguistically legitimate variety of American English and not a bastardization or "dumbing down" of English. Given the amount of time and effort linguists of every stripe have spent on legitimizing this variety—from observing speech, comparing systematic linguistic rules across dialects, and providing expert witness in cases of educational, employment, and housing discrimination—they would appreciate some respect on this issue by seeing public discourse avoid comments about African American English as code for racism. Second, the public needs to recognize that hearing difference isn't prejudice. It is clear from the research that our brains are wired to hear differences by groups at a fairly low level of cognitive processing. This gets back to the basics of Nash's group differentiation; hearing someone as sounding black or white is a normal reflection of group affiliation by the individual. However, using perceived vocal qualities as a proxy for race and then discriminating on the basis of that (by not returning phone calls, for example) is morally wrong. Finally, the educational system still needs to help in bridging home languages (e.g., Spanish, Hmong) and home dialects with what is taught in schools. Educators are subject to public opinion and the need to produce flashy research, leaving parents in the lurch as far as understanding their methods and approaches goes. Our hope is that discussions generated by this book will help sort out what is most helpful for the children, location by location, across Wisconsin.

CHAPTER 8

Hmong in Wisconsin

SUSAN MEREDITH BURT

This chapter first gives a brief overview of Hmong immigration and resulting demographics, then discusses the results of a research project on the influence of English on Hmong usage of Wisconsin Hmong Americans. The final section focuses on institutional responses to the ongoing language shift situation that constitutes the sociolinguistic reality facing Wisconsin Hmong Americans today.

Most accounts of Hmong people in Wisconsin and Minnesota (Hillmer 2009, Koltyk 1997, Lo 2001) date the arrival of the first Hmong refugees in the Upper Midwest to 1975 or 1976. Fungchatou Lo (2001, 104–5) describes subsequent waves of Hmong refugees, each of which added to the overall Hmong population of the state, which Lo pegged at 46,600 in 2000 (2001, 107). Mark Pfeifer's summary of 2006 census data from the American Community Survey gives the Hmong population of Wisconsin as 38,949, a smaller total, but whatever the actual number, Wisconsin ranks as the state with the third highest number of Hmong Americans in the country, behind only California and Minnesota. As is well known, most Hmong immigrants came to the United States via refugee camps in Thailand in the aftermath of the war in Southeast Asia. The language the refugees brought with them, also called Hmong, has several varieties, the most prominent of which are White Hmong and Green Hmong (a reference to the prevailing colors of traditional garb).

The Hmong language is argued by some to be a member of the Sino-Tibetan family, which would thus make Hmong related to Chinese; others argue that Hmong belongs to the Austro-Asiatic family, which would mean it was related to Vietnamese and Khmer (Ratliff 1997); in recent work, Martha Ratliff (2010) argues that the Hmong-Mien family is not Sino-Tibetan and that most Chinese lexical items in Hmong-Mien languages are the result of borrowing over a long period of contact. Still, she explicitly states that the question of the ultimate relationship between the two families remains open (2010, 240).

Most immigrants to English-speaking countries find that their children and grandchildren shift to English and may not even acquire the heritage language. Calvin Veltman (1983) has documented the rapidity of the shift to English monolingual status for many immigrant groups in the United States and claims that a complete shift takes as little as three generations (see chapters 2, 3, and 9 for discussion of other communities in Wisconsin). However, Michael Clyne (1991), writing about immigrant languages in Australia, another English-speaking country, gives a slightly different picture: in his data, immigrants from northern European countries, speaking languages like Dutch or German and sharing many cultural traits with English speakers, shift to English most rapidly, while immigrants to Australia who speak Southeast Asian languages like Khmer, Lao, or Vietnamese are more likely to retain their heritage languages. In contrast, Miranda Wilkerson and Joseph Salmons (2008) show that nineteenth-century German-speaking immigrants to Wisconsin did not shift as rapidly to English as today's immigrants do. Given these facts, it is not obvious whether we should expect Hmong Americans in Wisconsin to retain their heritage language or to abandon Hmong as they learn English.

It is unfortunate that no one has yet undertaken a multigenerational survey of Hmong language use in Wisconsin. But we can still ask what indicators are available that can tell us whether Hmong Americans are in the process of shifting entirely to English or whether they are working to set up mechanisms for retention of Hmong. Pfeifer's look at census data offers such indicators. For example, the Hmong population in the United States as a whole is a young population, with a median age of 19.1 years, compared with a much older median age of

36.4 years for the general population. Furthermore, 80 percent of Hmong Americans live in "family households" with children under the age of eighteen, while only 31.3 percent of the general population of the country lives in such households. According to the census, the average size of a Hmong family is 5.53 people whereas the average family size of the general population is only 3.2 people. Residence in a family, of course, provides the best opportunity for parents and grandparents to transmit the heritage language to children (though it does not guarantee, of course, that those children will retain the language). The census tells us further that of the population over the age of thirty, 15.4 percent of Hmong Americans live with their grandchildren, while only 3.5 percent of the general population does (table 8.1 shows a comparison of these demographic traits). With 55.7 percent of the Hmong American population having been born in the United States, Hmong parents and grandparents have a large number of children to whom the Hmong language can be transmitted. The census shows further that only 5.8 percent of Hmong Americans over the age of five speak only English and that 94.2 percent speak a language other than English. A total of 42.6 percent of the Hmong American population claim to speak English "less than very well" (Pfeifer 2006) (see figs. 8.1 and 8.2).

These figures suggest that Hmong Americans live in larger and more multigenerational households than most other Americans and that in most of these households Hmong is spoken. Pfeifer also interprets these data as showing "the strong priority Hmong families place

TABLE 8.1. Comparison of Hmong Americans and general U.S. population

Trait	Hmong Americans	General U.S. population
median age	19.1 years	36.4 years
living with children < 18	80%	31.3%
average family size	5.53 people	3.2 people
persons > 30 living with grandchildren	15.4%	3.5%

Source: Pfeifer 2006.

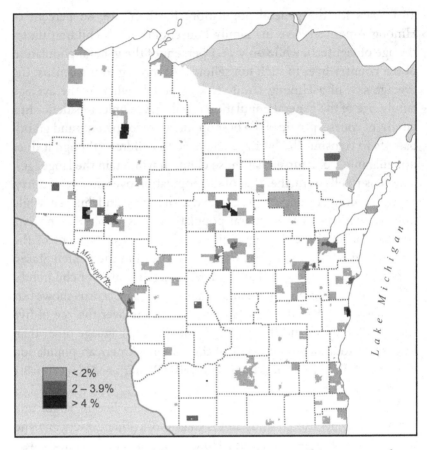

FIGURE 8.1. Percentage of people speaking Hmong at home in 2000, by county subdivision (Data from the 2000 U.S. census, table QTP16, "Language Spoken at Home," which is sample data. Percentages are the number of speakers per the total population aged five years and older.)

on maintaining the Hmong language among their children" (2006, 1). This picture is in accord with the qualitative view of the Hmong given by sociologist Jeremy Hein (2006). Hein compared the cultural adaptation of Hmong and Cambodian immigrants in cities large and small across the Upper Midwest. Hmong participants from Eau Claire and Milwaukee were contrasted with Cambodian participants from Rochester, Minnesota, and Chicago. Hein argues that the Hmong maintain

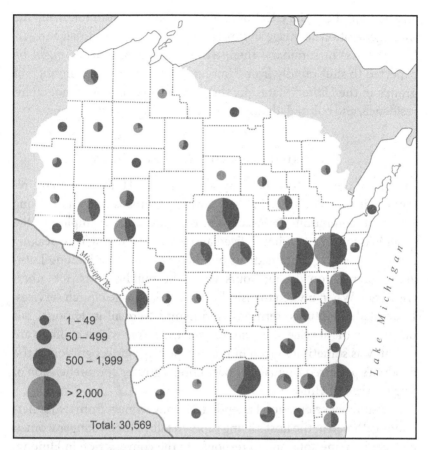

FIGURE 8.2. Number of people speaking Hmong at home in 2000, by county (Data from the 2000 U.S. census, table PCT010, "Age by Language Spoken at Home for the Population 5 Years and Over." The absence of a symbol for a particular county indicates that no Hmong speakers were reported there in 2000. Darker shading in the circle suggests the percentage of Hmong speakers eighteen and older; lighter shading indicates the percentage of speakers aged five to seventeen years.)

a more "hermetic" ethnic boundary than the Cambodians; in other words, if Hein is correct, Hmong Americans are more concerned with maintaining a distinctive Hmong identity in the United States than they are with assimilating culturally. This concern for maintaining their culture can, of course, extend to a desire to maintain their language, and perhaps it has the effect of preventing Hmong from following the three-generation language shift pattern delineated by Veltman and earlier scholars. In summary, then, while Hmong Americans *might* be expected to shift rapidly from Hmong to English, as many immigrant groups in the United States do, there are also factors of demography, residence, and cultural identity that may aid language retention.

BILINGUALISM AND LANGUAGE SHIFT

In spite of these factors that may serve to favor Hmong language retention, it is evident that English is making inroads into the Hmong American community in Wisconsin. Here are some examples: in the small Wisconsin city where I lived and worked, one English-speaking Lutheran congregation made its building available to a Hmong Lutheran congregation during hours when the building was not otherwise used. When invited to visit the Hmong-language church services, I attended; scriptures, sermons, and hymns were all in Hmong, but one part of the service, the *qhia menyuam*, a part in which children are taught, was sometimes given in English, perhaps in recognition of the children's preferred language or of children's greater comprehension of English than of Hmong.

At a summer celebration I attended, Hmong women from two generations gathered in the host's living room to talk. Three younger women collected on one sofa, and in response to the conversation in Hmong, one said under her breath, "Can you speak English?" They were clearly more comfortable with conversation in English than in Hmong.

For my research on the effects of English on Hmong, I was able to conduct language-focused interviews with thirty Hmong Americans, ten of whom met the experiential criterion I set for being called an "elder" for the purposes of the study: they had already had one child at the time of immigration. The twenty other speakers were college age, eighteen to twenty-six years old; all were recruited through the social network of my Hmong American research collaborator, Hua Yang. As a preliminary measure, we asked all thirty to assess their own knowledge of both English and Hmong on a six-point scale: none, beginner, fair, good, almost native, and native. Four of the elders

(40 percent) claimed to have no English; three (30 percent) rated themselves as beginners, and three (30 percent) rated themselves as fair in the knowledge of English. All ten elders were native speakers of Hmong (Burt 2010, 14).

Seven of the twenty young adults (35 percent) rated their Hmong as fair, four (20 percent) as good, seven (35 percent) as almost native, and only two (10 percent) as native. These young adults also rated their English: two (10 percent) as fair, three (15 percent) as good, six (30 percent) as almost native, and nine (45 percent) as native. Only one of the young adults rated herself as a native speaker of both Hmong and English, while two of the younger speakers rated themselves as almost native in both languages (Burt 2010, 14–15). These percentages are of a very small sample of speakers and should not be taken as representative, but they are suggestive. The fact that only two of the younger speakers consider themselves native speakers of Hmong while nine of them consider themselves native speakers of English can certainly be taken as evidence of language shift in progress. But there are more subtle ways in which contact with English can be seen to have affected the Hmong language: the next section shows how English-language usage has affected Hmong-language usage in the younger generation of speakers, in a way that could conceivably accelerate breakdown in intergenerational communication in Hmong.

Language Shift and Pragmatic Change

It is possible to see language shift as a series of choices: in any given interaction with other bilinguals, a bilingual speaker makes a choice whether to use Hmong or English or a combination thereof to speak to other people in the conversation. Obvious constraints on this choice include the extent of the speaker's own repertoire in both languages and the speaker's knowledge about the other people's repertoires or preferences. But there are other factors as well; one significant consideration is the reaction to any particular choice a speaker may get from those other people in the conversation. A negative or unhappy reaction can serve to taint that particular choice of language and perhaps lead the speaker not to choose the same language the next time.

Every language seems to have linguistic resources available to convey to listeners that the speaker means them no harm or wishes to show respect: we recognize these resources as tools to convey politeness. However, languages differ not only in what the politeness resources are but also in when and how they are implemented. Bilinguals, growing up with two languages, each with its own politeness system and politeness resources, may find it practical to merge the two systems rather than keep them apart. There is evidence that this has happened with Hmong and English in Wisconsin.

Perhaps the most familiar politeness resource in American English is the particle *please*; Jean Gleason, Rivka Perlmann, and Esther Greif (1984) show how American English-speaking adults rehearse this particle with their own children and with other children. Ten college-age speakers of American English were asked to formulate 14 requests each in the course of interviews, and the results were 51 instances of *please* in the 140 requests (Burt 2009, 2010). The Hmong-language version of the same interview script was given to ten Hmong elders in Wisconsin: in these responses, several different politeness particles surfaced, including *os, seb, soj, thov,* and *yom*. Only one of these, however, can be translated as "please," the particle *thov*; while the elders produced a total of 67 politeness particles in 140 requests, only 6 of those particles (less than 10 percent) were *thov*.

Twenty college-age Hmong American young adults participated in these interviews; ten were interviewed in Hmong and ten in English. The Hmong American young adults interviewed in English produced twenty instances of *please*, while the ten who were interviewed in Hmong produced exactly twenty instances of *thov* (and forty-six other particles for a total of sixty-six politeness particles). We can interpret these numbers as indicating that the young adult speakers had created a compromise politeness system for requests; rather than use *please* as often as native speakers of English do or use *thov* as infrequently as native speakers of Hmong do, the young Hmong American adults seem to have settled on an intermediate frequency for both their languages.

How, then, do older Hmong speakers react to requests spoken by younger speakers who use this mixed system? Some Hmong elders who took part in the study expressed their frustration with younger speakers' ways of speaking Hmong. Most Hmong speakers surveyed (in both generations) noted that it could be considered inappropriate for younger adult speakers to make requests of older relatives. But one younger speaker claimed that a request in Hmong that included *thov* would be acceptable, just as requests in English with *please* are. One elder seemed to have heard such requests from younger speakers—and she did not approve! She said, "Yog tus uas nws paubtap lawm mas nws kuj tsis nug; yog tsis paubtab ces lawm kuj yuav nug thiab" (If one is knowledgeable, s/he will not ask; if not knowledgeable, they will ask you) (Burt 2010, 98).[1]

Survey responses cannot tell us whether elders who disapprove of younger speakers' Hmong usage actually convey their disapproval in interaction, but it seems nonetheless possible that a younger speaker whose bilingual politeness system includes influences from American English could incur the disapproval of older speakers of Hmong. If elderly disapproval of their Hmong were communicated to them, younger speakers might decide that speaking Hmong was too unre-warding to attempt again with these elders.

Thus, usage differences between Hmong and English have at least the potential to lead to interactions in which speakers of different generations interpret the other speaker's usage as impolite, even if no impoliteness was intended. If such interactions render intergenerational communication in Hmong frustrating, the primary mechanism for maintaining Hmong as a community language could be weakened. Burt and Yang (2005) suggest that ESL instruction for Hmong students should alert English learners to these differences; heritage language instruction in Hmong could also include calling learners' attention to these differences. The next section explores possible opportunities for this.

INSTITUTIONAL RESPONSES TO HMONG LANGUAGE MATTERS

Further evidence of the bilingual, shifting language situation for Hmong in Wisconsin comes from institutional responses to it. The Wisconsin Department of Public Instruction (DPI) conducts an annual census of children in the public schools whose first language is not English. The most recent of these reports available, "March 2010 Census of Limited-English Proficient Pupils in Wisconsin by Language," dated March 2010, gave an overall count of 52,100 children.[2] Of these, 10,081 were Hmong speaking, amounting to 19.3 percent of the total number of children for whom English is not the first language. The Wisconsin DPI clearly recognizes the need for schools to provide instruction in English as a second language for these immigrant children, and lists eight public universities and six private ones in the state where prospective teachers can earn certification in teaching English as a second language. The DPI makes further helpful material available to public schools on its website, including a booklet designed to educate teachers and administrators on the needs of the most recent wave of Hmong immigration, those Hmong who took refuge in the Wat Tham Krabok monastery in Thailand rather than be repatriated to Laos, who were finally permitted to come to the United States in 2003. Half of this group was expected to be under the age of fourteen, so the DPI website provides information to help schools welcome these children. It is heartening to compare this institutional attempt to welcome and support Hmong immigrant families with the historical language and culture eradication efforts practiced against Native Americans as Monica Macaulay and Karen Washinawatok recount in chapter 1. Perhaps we have learned something.

Support for the heritage language in the form of instruction in Hmong, however, is much more difficult to come by. The pastor and the president of the Hmong Lutheran congregation that befriended me collaborated to offer informal Hmong-language instruction both to adolescents within the congregation (heritage learners) and to English-speaking adults who wanted to learn Hmong. Both men have now moved away from that small city, but there may be other individual small-scale attempts to teach the language in the state. The DPI website lists twelve languages that are taught in Wisconsin schools; these include local heritage languages such as Ojibwe, Menominee, German, Norwegian, and Spanish, as well as American Sign Language, and global languages such as Chinese, French, Hebrew, Japanese, and Russian, but Hmong has not yet made it onto the list. According to one source, the Appleton school district has offered Hmong-language instruction on

Saturdays, but not as much as some students want (Don Hones, personal communication). Again, we can contrast the heritage language educational resources available to Hmong immigrants with the richness of those that were offered to German-speaking Wisconsin children in the nineteenth century (see chapter 3) and hope that opportunities for Hmong language education will grow.

Several public universities in Wisconsin, however, have developed courses to support Hmong language and culture. The University of Wisconsin–Oshkosh offers a course in Hmong language, culture, and learning, which is open to both Hmong American students and students of other ethnic backgrounds. The Linguistics Department of the University of Wisconsin–Milwaukee offers a course in Hmong language literacy for speakers of Hmong.[3] The most extensive support is available at the University of Wisconsin–Madison, where six semesters of Hmong-language instruction are available during summers and the academic year. While these courses are largely geared toward heritage learners, nonheritage learners can also enroll.

It might be asked, however, whether these efforts are sufficient for maintaining Hmong as a living, spoken language in Wisconsin, assuming (as I do) that the Hmong American community believes that heritage language maintenance is a social goal worth pursuing. It is clear that American English has already had some influence on the way that younger Hmong Americans speak Hmong. But Hmong can perhaps still survive and thrive as a community language if differences I have described here between the immigrant generation's use of Hmong and younger speakers' use of Hmong can be recognized as differences that arise from different social conditions and learning conditions rather than as character deficiencies on the part of one generation of speakers or the other. Hopefully, greater availability of Hmong instruction and addressing generational differences in that instruction can make speaking Hmong in Wisconsin more rewarding for all.

NOTES

1. The Romanized Popular Alphabet (RPA), used here, is the system of writing Hmong that is most widely used in the United States. Created by

missionaries in Laos in the 1950s, it represents nasalized vowels as doubled vowels; thus, *oo* represents open *o* followed by a velar nasal. The eight tones of the language are represented by consonant letters at the end of the syllable in this otherwise strictly consonant-vowel language. Thus, *Hmong* is spelled *Hmoob*, with the *b* representing a high tone.

2. See http://ell.dpi.wi.gov/files/ell/pdf/elp-lang-2010.pdf.

3. Duffy 2007 demonstrates how scarce opportunities for literacy instruction were in Laos.

CHAPTER 9

Spanish in Wisconsin

Advantages of Maintenance and Prospects for Sustained Vitality

CATHERINE STAFFORD

In this chapter I focus on the perhaps surprising linguistic diversity of Wisconsin's Hispanic population. After a brief demographic overview of Spanish speakers in the state, I highlight some of the many advantages of the highly proficient bilingualism enjoyed by some—but certainly not all—of Wisconsin's Hispanics and argue that it is more beneficial at individual, community, and societal levels to promote highly proficient Spanish-English bilingualism than it is to replace the Spanish they already know, use, and value with English. Within this context, I discuss the multileveled commitment that is required to develop and maintain highly proficient bilingualism among not only Hispanics but also speakers of any non-English language that is marked undeservedly by lower social status and currency in our culture. Finally, I offer an outlook for the continued vitality of Spanish as a minority language in Wisconsin.[1]

WHO ARE WISCONSIN HISPANICS?

The U.S. Census Bureau estimates that in 2009 there were 299,123 Hispanics in the state of Wisconsin, comprising approximately 5 percent of the total population of the state. This figure represents a 55 percent increase from the 2000 census, according to which the Hispanic population of Wisconsin was 192,921. While it is currently concentrated in the southeastern part of the state and in urban areas, according to census data the Hispanic population has been growing in every county in Wisconsin. Hispanics make up more than 5 percent of the total population of eight Wisconsin counties; in both Racine and Kenosha counties Hispanics comprise 10 percent of the population, and in Milwaukee County they account for 12 percent of the population.[2] According to the Pew Hispanic Center, the Hispanic population grew by more than 100 percent in forty-six of Wisconsin's seventy-two counties between 1990 and 2000, and in seven counties between 2000 and 2008. In six of these seven latter counties, Hispanics still account for just 1 or 2 percent of the total county population, meaning that the most recent rapid-growth areas across the state still include relatively few Hispanics in the total citizenry (see fig. 9.1).[3] These numbers are consequential; as both Karen Washinawatok and Monica Macaulay's and Antje Petty's respective discussions in chapters 1 and 3 of this volume make clear, there is a complex interplay of factors—including population density—involved in ensuring the continued vitality of minority languages and cultures.

Despite the size and steady growth of this minority community, it is a particularly vulnerable sector of Wisconsin's population in many respects. The median income among Hispanics is less than that of both non-Hispanic whites and non-Hispanic blacks. Of Hispanics aged seventeen years or younger, 23 percent live in poverty; of those between the ages of eighteen and sixty-four, 18 percent live in poverty.

Hispanic children tend also to be at an educational disadvantage, particularly relative to their non-Hispanic white peers. According to the Alliance for Excellent Education, the overall high school graduation rate in the state of Wisconsin for the 2005–6 school year was 82 percent, among the best rates in the country. The graduation rate among Wisconsin's Hispanic students, however, was just 54 percent, representing a sizeable achievement gap. Data from the 2000 census similarly indicate that Wisconsin Hispanics lag behind state averages in ultimate educational attainment (summarized in fig. 9.2). While just 5 percent of all Wisconsin residents had attained less than a ninth-grade education, a full 25 percent of the state's Hispanics had. The proportion of all residents who had earned a high school diploma or equivalency with

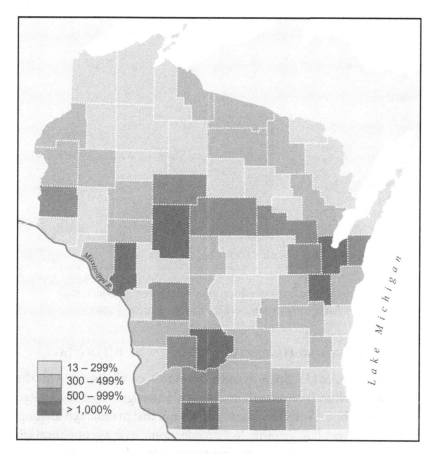

FIGURE 9.1. Percentage change in Hispanic population, 1990–2010, by county (Data computed from statistics from the 1990 and 2010 U.S. censuses for Hispanics of "any race")

no further schooling was 34 percent, but just 24 percent among Hispanics, and while 22 percent of all Wisconsin residents held a bachelor's degree or higher, only 11 percent of Hispanics did. A grave consequence of such educational—and concomitant economic—disadvantage is the unjust social stigmatization of both Wisconsin Hispanics and their language, which, as linguist and bilingual education specialist Joshua Fishman (2001, 2006) has pointed out, creates obstacles for the recognition of minority languages like U.S. Spanish as the rich and valuable linguistic traditions they are and makes it difficult to maintain them.

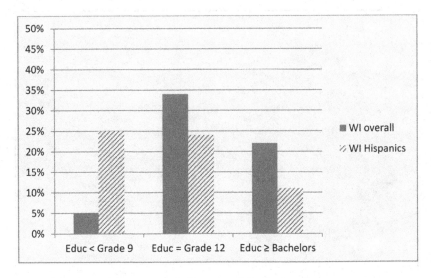

FIGURE 9.2. Comparisons of educational attainment between state averages and Wisconsin Hispanics (U.S. Census Bureau 2000)

WHY SHOULD HISPANICS STRIVE TO BE BILINGUAL?

Stigmatization of U.S. Spanish contributes to societal disregard for the invaluable cultural, economic, and political strengths that the United States could boast with a Hispanic population that maintained lifelong, highly proficient bilingualism. In a broader context, the geopolitical climate since September 11, 2001, has brought to the fore how crucially important expertise in non-English languages is to the nation's interests. This awareness has emerged most especially in the context of the United States' urgent need to engage with other countries in more culturally sensitive and constructive ways. Many secondary schools, colleges, and universities make study of a foreign language a graduation requirement.[4] Anglophone students who satisfy these requirements commonly exit foreign-language programs with some reading, writing, and comprehension knowledge, but unfortunately, highly proficient oral skills and cultural knowledge are far less common. At the same time, the United States is home to considerable numbers of heritage speakers, or individuals who grow up speaking or at least hearing their families' non-English language at home, and those heritage speakers who are raised bilingual possess unique linguistic and cultural competencies that, if allowed to flourish, could be a tremendously beneficial resource on the geopolitical stage.

Moreover, bilingualism research in the last three decades has found that highly proficient, lifelong bilingualism confers cognitive advantages that, interestingly, reach beyond language skill to include enhanced creative thinking, mental flexibility, and capacity to focus one's attention in the face of distraction. Research also suggests that bilingualism can help to protect against cognitive decline that occurs with normal aging.

WHAT STANDS IN THE WAY OF HIGHLY PROFICIENT BILINGUALISM IN THE UNITED STATES?

Unfortunately, the predominant language policy in the U.S. education system is one that disregards the many advantages that stand to be gained from both individual bilingualism and a multilingual, multicultural populace and that makes English the exclusive language of instruction in content areas like math and history, with some classroom instruction in foreign languages offered at the secondary level. A devastating consequence of these English-only policies for many children, Hispanics included, is the arrested development or complete loss of the non-English home language and thus the opportunity to become highly proficient bilinguals and thereby contribute to a much needed, institutionally supported, linguistic pluralism in the United States.

Language policies that favor educating children monolingually in English over developing and maintaining bilingualism are perhaps a vestige of misconceptions that grew out of research findings published in the xenophobic climate of the first half of the twentieth century. These ideologically tainted studies concluded that bilingualism meant imperfect mastery of two languages (referred to by some pejoratively as "semilingualism") and that it could lead to cognitive confusion, even schizophrenia, and was therefore to be avoided. Of course, these claims have long since been discredited, but unfortunately, the destructive, narrow-minded ideologies associated with them persist.

In recent years, researchers in bilingualism and advocates for ethnolinguistic minorities have argued assertively and convincingly that developing and maintaining highly proficient bilingualism among speakers of languages other than English is an outcome that is far more beneficial than supplanting heritage languages like U.S. Spanish with English. While developing and maintaining highly proficient bilingualism among ethnolinguistic minorities are certainly achievable goals, they are nevertheless complicated processes that demand committed collaboration among multiple stakeholders.

U.S. Hispanics are a complex, linguistically diverse population. To begin with, given Hispanic immigrants' varied countries of origin, the United States has become a unique melting pot for numerous regional varieties of Spanish. These varieties are mutually intelligible, but they present many phonetic, grammatical, and lexical differences that speakers often find themselves negotiating with other native Spanish speakers living in the same community. Moreover, individuals who self-identify or are identified as Hispanic include monolingual English speakers, monolingual Spanish speakers, and bilingual/multilingual individuals whose relative proficiency in Spanish, English, and in some cases Latin American indigenous languages varies widely. Census data illustrates the linguistic diversity of the Hispanic population in Wisconsin; for example, according to data from the 2000 census, 33 percent of Hispanics in Wisconsin aged five and older spoke only English at home, 66 percent spoke Spanish, and 1 percent spoke a language other than English or Spanish. Of those who reported speaking Spanish at home, 48 percent reported that they also spoke English "very well," 21 percent reported speaking it "well," 20 percent reported speaking it "not well," and 11 percent reported speaking no English (see fig. 9.3).

Equally varied are the resources available to Hispanics to develop and/or maintain high levels of proficiency in Spanish and English. Sadly, the false notion that bilingualism somehow runs counter to nationalism is invoked all too often when communities are shaping language and education policies, with damaging results for ethnolinguistic minorities like Wisconsin's Hispanics. In what follows, I discuss some of the policies and practices of families, school systems, and society at large, offering commentary along the way on the opportunities and challenges that these policies and practices present for the development

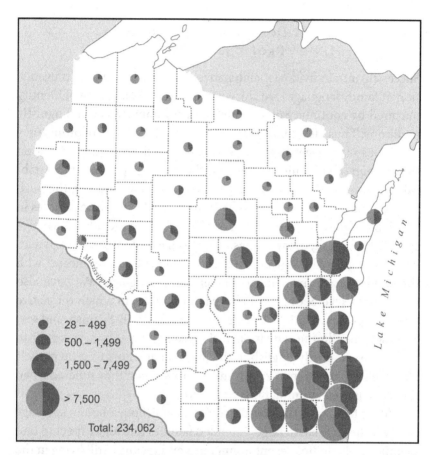

Legend:
- 28 – 499
- 500 – 1,499
- 1,500 – 7,499
- > 7,500

Total: 234,062

FIGURE 9.3. Number of Spanish speakers, 2006–10, by county (Data from the American Community Survey 2006–7, five-year estimates, table DP02, "Selected Social Characteristics in the United States." Darker shading in the circle suggests the percentage of Spanish speakers who reported speaking English less than "very well" as a percentage of the total number of Spanish speakers for that particular county.)

and maintenance of balanced bilingualism among Wisconsin's Hispanics and across the United States in general.

What Does It Take to Promote Highly Proficient Bilingualism?

Successful intraindividual maintenance and intergenerational transmission of family languages are closely tied with a strong sense of identity nurtured by continuity of a family's and community's ethnolinguistic traditions. Thus, developing and maintaining high levels of proficiency in minority languages like U.S. Spanish depend first and foremost on the makeup of Hispanic families and the language policies they establish at home. These policies vary widely from one family to the next. For example, my research team has interviewed Wisconsin families in which one parent is a native speaker of Spanish and the other is a native speaker of English; many of these families have adopted a "one parent, one language" policy, meaning that each parent communicates with the children exclusively in his or her native language. We have also interviewed several one- and two-parent families in which the native Spanish-speaking parents have decided to speak only Spanish, and several more families in which Spanish-speaking parents have opted to speak only or mostly English in the home in an effort to protect their children from the stigmatization and discrimination they suffered when they first arrived as immigrants to Wisconsin.

Adding further to the complexity of establishing a family language policy is the fact that in large, extended families one may expect to find members—including recent immigrants and relatives still living in the home region—who speak that region's dialect of Spanish as well as U.S.-born family members who speak a distinct variety of U.S. Spanish. For instance, in their interviews with us, a brother and sister who arrived as young children to the mainland from Puerto Rico both expressed the strong sense of rejection they now feel when they go to Puerto Rico to visit their relatives, who poke fun at the "funny way" the siblings speak Spanish. Members of the same family at any given point in time are likely to have quite different proficiencies in Spanish, English, and perhaps indigenous languages like Mixtec, an American Indian language from southern Mexico that is spoken in a sizeable community in the Green Bay area. All the while, a family's—indeed a community's— intricate linguistic mosaic provides the backdrop against which children acquire the home language, acquisition that occurs in the informal, nontutored setting of day-to-day communication with family and community members.

If the children in linguistic minority communities grow up bilingual, their two languages are likely to serve complementary purposes, simply because daily life in the United States does not afford the same opportunities for bilinguals to use both their languages in all domains of use. Wisconsin Hispanics who participated in one of my recent studies commonly reported that they used Spanish most often at home, in church, and in other informal, community contexts and used English more often in academic and professional contexts. Given this situation of language development and use in distinct, nonoverlapping contexts, called "diglossia" by some researchers, a bilingual's competencies in either language tend to be very different, with the relative strength of his or her ability in the two languages being determined in large part by societal factors of prestige, power, and the perceived value of the languages in question.

Consequently, Hispanic children who have grown up in diglossic situations in the United States often enter school with solid mastery of informal, everyday usage of their families' varieties of Spanish, and with varied degrees of familiarity with academic usage of Spanish and English.[5] By contrast, some Hispanic families travel back and forth between the United States and their countries of origin. If families stay for extended periods of time in Spanish-speaking countries, children often attend schools where school subjects are taught in Spanish. Given their comparatively rich exposure to academic Spanish in non-U.S. schools, these children tend to enjoy high proficiency in the family language, proficiency that includes well-developed literacy skills and mastery of academic usage of Spanish.

Irrespective of early childhood experience, when Spanish-speaking children enroll in U.S. schools, they shift rapidly to often exclusive use of English, not only because it is mandated but also because it is the predominant language of their peer group and is therefore perceived as a key to acceptance by and participation in the majority community. Due to the reduced exposure to and use of Spanish that co-occur with the onset of their schooling in the United States, many Hispanic children experience a change in language dominance whereby they become less proficient in or even lose their native Spanish because it is displaced by English, the prestigious, high-currency societal language. For example, in a recent survey I conducted, out of a group of thirty Wisconsin Hispanic adults who were either born in the United States or moved here before school age, twenty-six said that their English skills were stronger than their Spanish skills. Of the other four, only one individual reported stronger proficiency in Spanish than in English; the remaining three said that their Spanish and English skills were comparably strong.

Turning back to the big picture, the linguistic diversity that stems from Hispanic children's varied experiences during the early years presents two important challenges for education. First, Hispanic children—and particularly older children—who enter school without age-appropriate literacy skills in either Spanish or English are at grave risk of falling behind in all academic content areas while they acquire the language skills necessary to be able to benefit from instruction that is delivered in English. Given that literacy is the keystone for successful academic development overall, the importance of overcoming this particular challenge cannot be overemphasized if we are committed to providing equality of educational opportunity for linguistic minority students like Wisconsin's Hispanic youth.

Second, children who enter school with limited English proficiency may speak Spanish dialects that are unfamiliar to nonnatives and/or scorned by native-speaker school personnel whose job is to provide support for students who are just beginning to learn English. If the nonacademic usage and stigmatized Spanish dialects these children speak are devalued—whether overtly or implicitly—young would-be bilinguals may adopt the view that the Spanish they have learned and use at home is somehow defective, perhaps leading to diminished personal connections with, negative attitudes about, and ultimately abandonment of their family language in favor of English. Thus, successful acquisition of what is referred to as "additive bilingualism," or high proficiency in both the societal and the family language, depends as much on institutional recognition of and respect for linguistic diversity as it does on development of proficiency and literacy in academic and professional usage of both Spanish and English.

While there is no doubt that high proficiency in English is essential for securing social acceptance, education, and upward mobility in Wisconsin and the United States at large, concurrent expertise in heritage languages like Spanish offers intellectual, cultural, economic, and diplomatic benefits at the individual, community, and societal levels. Therefore, the development of additive bilingualism among heritage speakers is clearly a more constructive goal than replacing heritage languages with English monolingualism. And it is a goal that requires a dedicated place for heritage language development and preservation on the national agenda along with the collaborative involvement of individuals, their families, communities, educators, and policy makers.

The present structure of the U.S. public education system provides two main options for supporting Hispanic students who wish to develop, maintain, or reacquire Spanish as part of efforts to become highly proficient bilinguals. These options are to enroll either in maintenance bilingual education programs or in classes in which Spanish is taught as a foreign language. The latter option is more widely available owing to the current predominant curricular structure of U.S. schools. Maintenance bilingual education programs, the notably less common option, use Spanish as the language of instruction in a number of subject areas either after or at the same time that Spanish-speaking Hispanic students are acquiring English. These programs, whose ultimate goal is biliterate bilingualism, are designed to provide instructional and institutional support for Hispanic students so that they not only develop highly proficient English skills but also develop, maintain, or reacquire Spanish. This is the stated mission of Milwaukee Public School's Spanish-English bilingual programming, which at the time of writing was offered in sixteen elementary schools, four middle schools, and four high schools.[6]

One such bilingual education model is known as dual language immersion.[7] These programs, also known as two-way bilingual programs, enroll native speakers of both Spanish and English, typically starting in kindergarten. During the first year in the program, elementary-level students receive instruction in Spanish for 90 percent of the school day and in English for 10 percent of the school day. As students advance through the program, the proportion of instruction delivered in Spanish and English is gradually leveled so that by grade 4 or 5 they are using each language for 50 percent of the school day.

Unfortunately, despite the increased popularity and success of maintenance bilingual education like dual immersion programs (see chapter 1 for discussion of similar immersion programs designed for speakers of Wisconsin's Native American languages), the goals of developing highly proficient English on the one hand and maintaining heritage languages on the other continue to be viewed by and large as an either/or proposition. This erroneous assumption may be fueled by the prevailing—and likewise erroneous—belief that being a monolingual Anglophone is a mark of good citizenship and that therefore bilingualism is somehow incompatible with nationalism. A common consequence of the perceived necessity to choose between fluency in the societal or the heritage language is referred to as "subtractive bilingualism"; in this scenario, development of proficiency in English comes at the cost of arrested development and loss of heritage languages.

Transitional bilingual programs, which remain the predominant model of bilingual education in U.S. school systems, are an example of how established education policy institutionalizes subtractive bilingualism. Under the transitional model of bilingual education (which is not really bilingual education at all given that its desired outcome is English monolingualism), Hispanic students who are English-language learners may—but don't always—receive initial educational support in Spanish, but the objective is for students to make as rapid a transition as possible to schooling in English only, usually in the space of two or three years. In addition to institutionally upholding subtractive bilingualism, this damaging education policy aligns poorly with language acquisition research like that of Jim Cummins, whose findings indicate that while two years may be sufficient to develop functional social use of a second language (e.g., for Spanish-speaking Hispanic children to speak English with their Anglophone classmates at recess), five years of study is a minimal requirement for the development of functional academic use (e.g., for Spanish-speaking Hispanic children to benefit from instruction delivered in English). Therefore, not only does the typical two- or three-year transitional program coerce abandonment of what would be highly beneficial bilingualism for language minority students like Hispanics but it also is not designed to adequately prepare them to succeed academically as functionally proficient and literate users of English, as the above-mentioned statistics related to the Hispanic achievement gap in Wisconsin strongly suggest. Statistics like these lay bare the underlying issues of equity in education for minority students in Wisconsin and indeed across the United States.

As noted at the beginning of this chapter, regions of Wisconsin that are currently experiencing rapid growth in Hispanic populations still have low absolute numbers of Hispanics. This means that there is not the "critical mass" of Spanish-speaking students needed to support widespread establishment of maintenance bilingual education programs, including Spanish classes designed specifically for heritage speakers.[8] The result is that more and more traditional Spanish classes (i.e., in which Spanish is taught as a foreign language) in secondary schools, colleges, and universities are opening their doors to heritage Spanish speakers seeking to reacquire or maintain or to further develop their family language. However, while the extension of existing resources in this way to provide Spanish instruction for heritage speakers is a necessary compromise in a time of ubiquitous budget cuts, the vastly different linguistic and educational needs of heritage Spanish speakers make their placement within the traditional sequence of courses in Spanish as a foreign language (SFL) complicated if not downright imprudent.

First, there are important qualitative differences between the linguistic knowledge of heritage speakers who learn Spanish as young children and that of monolingual English speakers who begin learning SFL as adolescents. Moreover, as I've detailed, the range and depth of heritage speakers' language skills may vary widely with their individual experiences at the time that they enroll in U.S. school systems. For example, a heritage speaker's oral Spanish may be highly fluent, seeming to justify placement in an advanced SFL class. At the same time, however, gaps in the same student's grammatical knowledge or writing skills may make placement in a first-year Spanish class seem warranted. Given the diversity in language competencies commonly found among heritage Spanish speakers, placement guidelines used for Anglophone SFL students clearly are not adequate for the purposes of placing heritage Spanish speakers appropriately in an SFL sequence.

To solve this placement dilemma, proper diagnostic tools must be developed to assess the specific skills and needs of heritage speakers. The design of these tools must have as its foundation a solid understanding of how heritage speakers' linguistic knowledge is both structured and used. After all, heritage speakers are particular kinds of bilinguals, and the linguistic knowledge of bilinguals is by definition qualitatively different from that of monolinguals. Therefore, it is more appropriate to assess heritage speakers' language competences vis-à-vis those of other bilinguals rather than those of monolingual Spanish or English speakers. Diagnostic tools must be capable moreover of assessing literacy skills and degree of mastery of different varieties of Spanish, skills that vary widely among heritage speakers. The American Council of Teachers of Foreign Languages recognized over a decade ago that heritage language learners have skills and instructional needs that are distinct from those of foreign-language learners, but the creation of adequate diagnostic and instructional resources that align properly with heritage learners' skills and needs is still very much a work in progress.

If the task of placing heritage language students in existing SFL programs can be accomplished satisfactorily, language-teaching professionals must then meet the instructional challenge of reaching both the Anglophones and the heritage Spanish speakers in their mixed-ability Spanish classes. Having learned Spanish as young children, heritage speakers possess linguistic knowledge that is primarily implicit and unconscious. Traditional SFL classes, however, are designed for explicit SFL learning and rely on instructional methods that, while a good fit for the native English speakers who make up the majority of students in SFL classes, are at odds with heritage speakers' implicit linguistic knowledge. For example, while traditional SFL students may have to memorize lists that commonly appear in introductory Spanish textbooks of the different uses of *ser* and *estar*, the two Spanish verbs that mean *to be*, heritage speakers are likely to have mature command of the appropriate usage of these verbs but not the ability to explain why their perfect usage is perfect ("It just sounds right!"). For assessment purposes, it may be pedagogically sound to quiz SFL students on the uses of *ser* and *estar* as they begin to learn how to use the verbs appropriately in writing and speaking, but requiring this same sort of explicit, metalinguistic explanation of heritage speakers is ill suited to their implicit linguistic knowledge and certainly does not allow them to further develop their existing language skills in any meaningful way.

An even more fundamental conclusion that we may draw from the foregoing example is that we need to develop methods and curricula for heritage speakers based on principled and coherent theories of how heritage language development proceeds in a classroom context, particularly given the fact that many Hispanic students' acquisition of Spanish up to this point will have occurred in informal settings at home and in the community. Current theories of how monolingual adolescents successfully learn foreign languages are not likely to be entirely (if at all) applicable to heritage language learning.

Furthermore, instructional approaches must be sensitive to the as-yet poorly understood cognitive differences that exist between heritage speakers whose linguistic profiles upon entering school vary with their early childhood experiences with language learning and use. Depending on these experiences, heritage speakers may be variously acquiring particular features of Spanish for the first time, continuing acquisition of features that had not yet developed to maturity before enrollment in school brought rapid transition to primary use of English, or relearning previously acquired features of Spanish that they have lost due to reduced exposure to Spanish in daily interpersonal communication and fewer opportunities to use it. Still other heritage speakers may have well-developed comprehension skills but are not yet able to use the language productively. In short, the design of instruction for such a diverse linguistic population must be responsive to heritage speakers' status as bilinguals with varied levels of fluency, literacy, and mastery of each of the linguistic subsystems (e.g., pronunciation, word forms and sentence structures, vocabulary, and norms of language use) in all varieties and usages of Spanish that are relevant to the student population being served.

Language instruction in both Spanish and English should consider not only heritage speakers' current needs but also their future aspirations. Moreover, in view of the advantages of bilingualism, instruction for heritage learners should seek to capitalize on the knowledge and skills that these bilinguals already possess and expand their linguistic repertoires to include as many varieties as are needed for heritage speakers to function successfully in both Spanish and English in the broadest possible range of social, academic, and professional contexts.

The provision of differentiated instruction in mixed SFL classes is one compelling possibility for reaching all students in heterogeneous classes that include SFL and heritage Spanish speakers. This teaching methodology, developed by Carol Ann Tomlinson, includes instructional techniques such as learning stations, personal agendas, learning contracts, and journals. This inventive, complex, and labor-intensive instructional method requires dedicated collaboration and resources, including school administrators who are understanding of heritage speakers and the unique talents and needs they bring to the classroom, experienced faculty and/or teacher training to reach students across the broad range of SFL and heritage Spanish speakers, and curricular materials designed to meet the learning needs of both SFL and heritage students.

If the nation's schools commit to accomplishing these goals of providing institutional support for the development of highly proficient bilinguals, then the future vitality of minority languages like U.S. Spanish may yet be bright. In the following section I address a number of other conditions that must be met to assure a minority language's survival and assess the state of affairs for the continued vitality of Spanish in Wisconsin.

How Does the Future Look for Spanish in Wisconsin?

In light of the foregoing discussion of social, political, and educational factors involved in the successful maintenance of a minority language like U.S. Spanish, it becomes clear that population growth such as that which is occurring among Wisconsin's Hispanics is no guarantee that Spanish will thrive in the face of pressure to integrate—integration here being understood in the more extreme sense of abandoning the Spanish language and Hispanic culture—in the name of good citizenship. Factors that have been shown to favor successful preservation of minority languages include the proportion of youth in the community, active use of the minority language at home and in the community, a steady influx of immigrants to the community, and education policy that promotes additive bilingualism. State trends related to the first two of these variables bode well for the continued vitality of Spanish in Wisconsin; trends related to the other two variables, however, may contribute to undermining the vitality of Spanish across the state.

With regard to the more promising trends, first, according to 2008 estimates, the median age of Wisconsin Hispanics was a youthful twenty-five, similar to the median age of the state's Hmong Americans noted in chapter 8. In comparison, the median age of non-Hispanic whites in Wisconsin the same year was forty-one, and among non-Hispanic blacks the median age was twenty-eight. Second, the past decade has seen a slight proportional increase in use of Spanish at home (66 percent in 2000 and approximately 70 percent in 2008).[9]

At the same time, however, Wisconsin has seen a decrease in recent years in the proportion of immigrants that make up the state's Hispanic population (40 percent in 2000 and 34 percent in 2008). This decrease is consistent with predictions that U.S.-born Hispanics will be the driving force of future population growth among Wisconsin Hispanics, and it is a trend that represents a shift from the 1990s, when immigrants accounted for the lion's share of population growth among Hispanics in the state.

According to 2008 census estimates, 66 percent of Wisconsin Hispanics were the U.S.-born descendants of first-generation immigrants. Studies of intergenerational language transmission in minority communities have frequently found that by the third generation (i.e., grandchildren of immigrants), members of minority communities are commonly either more proficient speakers of the majority language than the immigrant language or else monolingual speakers of the majority language.

Consequently for U.S. Hispanics, Spanish ceases to be transmitted intergenerationally, meaning that younger generations within the Hispanic community are in danger of missing out on the cultural, economic, linguistic, and cognitive advantages of bilingualism. However, family, community and institutional support, and advocacy for additive bilingualism can ensure that Hispanics—and Hispanic youth in particular—across Wisconsin realize their potential as highly proficient users of both Spanish and English, thus preserving Spanish in Wisconsin as the invaluable linguistic, cultural, economic, and political resource that it is.

NOTES

1. Readers interested in learning more about Spanish in the United States might consult the work of Kim Potowski, Carmen Silva-Corvalán, and Ana Celia Zentella. Those interested in the development and maintenance of bilingualism might find the work of Jim Cummins, Joshua Fishman, François Grosjean, and Guadalupe Valdés to be helpful. Finally, Ellen Bialystok, Albert Costa, and their colleagues have published extensively on the advantages of bilingualism and are a valuable resource for interested readers. Representative works of many of these authors are included in the reference list at the end of this book.

2. Given the relative youth of Wisconsin's Hispanics, percentages are often higher in the school-age population. For example, according to district demographics reports for 2011–12, Hispanics make up 24.6 percent of the K-12 population in the Racine Unified School District, 24.9 percent in the Kenosha Unified School District, and 23.5 percent in Milwaukee Public Schools.

3. These counties are Calumet, Iowa, Kewaunee, Lafayette, Menominee, Sawyer, and Trempealeau.

4. Two years of study of a foreign language in high school is an admission requirement for the University of Wisconsin–Eau Claire and the University of Wisconsin–Madison, and it is strongly recommended for admission to the University of Wisconsin–Milwaukee. At all of the University of Wisconsin system's four-year campuses, at least two semesters of study of a foreign language are required for a bachelor of arts degree. Mount Mary College, Northland College, and Silver Lake College are the only four-year postsecondary institutions in Wisconsin for which foreign-language study is not a requirement for any degree program.

5. According to 2008 estimates reported by the Pew Hispanic Center, 79 percent of Wisconsin Hispanics are of Mexican descent. While this statistic may suggest a relatively homogeneous Spanish-speaking population, it is important

to note that it is impossible to speak of "Mexican Spanish" as a uniform language variety. (See chapter 6 on the differences in the varieties of American English spoken in the Upper Midwest, New England, and the Deep South, and the positive and negative attitudes associated with speakers of these dialects.) Add to that the fact that the other 21 percent of Wisconsin Hispanics speak non-Mexican varieties of Spanish and the linguistic landscape becomes all the more intricate.

6. According to the Milwaukee Public Schools website, its bilingual programs "are designed to preserve and develop the first language while ensuring full proficiency in English. Children are taught all subject areas in both English and Spanish. ESL is a component of bilingual programs" (http://www.milwau kee.k12.wi.us/portal/server.pt/comm/schools/315/bilingual_education/38 622#).

7. In addition to the well-established program in Milwaukee, at the time of writing there were bilingual programs of these types offered in the Green Bay, Madison, Racine, and Sheboygan public schools.

8. It is notable and encouraging, however, that Spanish courses for native/ heritage Spanish speakers are offered in school districts with larger Hispanic student populations. These districts include Appleton, Green Bay, Janesville, Kenosha, Racine, and Sheboygan. Within the University of Wisconsin system, Spanish classes for heritage speakers are offered at Madison, Milwaukee, Oshkosh, and Whitewater.

9. According to 1990 census data, of the 75,931 Hispanic Wisconsinites aged five and above who spoke Spanish at home, approximately 63 percent were reported to speak English at least "very well." Of the 168,778 Wisconsin residents aged five and above counted in the 2000 census, approximately 55 percent were reported to speak English at least "very well." Unfortunately, the 2008 estimates reported by the Pew Hispanic Center did not include similar data for English proficiency.

CHAPTER 10

Mapping Wisconsin's Linguistic Landscapes

MARK LIVENGOOD

O n a Sunday afternoon I walked west along the north shore of Lake Monona toward the state Capitol. It's a route I've walked often the past few years, and over time I've developed a better understanding of the local cultural landscape. Small plaques marking places of official significance have helped me to imagine how Madison has developed in the past 150 years. One plaque identifies an L-plan cottage as "a vestige of immigrant housing" in the former Third Lake Ridge Germanic community that thrived on the near east side in the late nineteenth century. Across U.S. 151 (built in 1926) and just up the drumlin another plaque marks the place a Sac warrior was killed in 1832, during the Black Hawk War. On the other side of the street is the former spot of O'Cayz Corral, the club where grunge rock bands Nirvana and Soundgarden played in the late 1980s before hitting the big time.

On that sunny afternoon, however, I was not searching for markers, buildings, and vacant lots that memorialize and reflect the city's history. I was looking, and listening, for another cultural resource, one of our most basic: language. A landscape, as geographer D. W. Meinig (1979, 43) suggests, is the "complex cumulative record of the work of nature" and humans. We plow the earth into cornfields, we construct houses, and we plan and pave streets. We also name subdivisions and erect signs. According to Rodrigue Landry and Richard Bourhis (1997, 25), this "language of public road signs, advertising billboards, street names, place names, commercial shop signs, and public signs on government buildings combines to form the linguistic landscape of a given territory, region, or urban agglomeration." Any landscape, however, is textured by stories, oral and written, old and new, and inflected by the diverse voices of its living inhabitants and visitors. A thorough definition of a linguistic landscape, therefore, should include the many forms of language that generate a place's particular linguistic character, whether that place is a town in Price County, a Milwaukee neighborhood, or a section of Madison.

I walked west through the former German enclave, brittle leaves crackling underfoot, and passed a man scraping paint from a house, a Spanish-language advertisement blaring from his radio. Along the bike path a cyclist had stopped to quench her thirst. She stood kitty-corner (or kitty-cross or kitty-wampus, depending on where you're from) from the Essen Haus restaurant and bar and the Germania gift shop, drinking from a device called (again depending on where you're from) a "bubbler," "drinking fountain," or "water fountain." From there, the bike path skirts the north shore of Lake Monona, a place name, according to *The Place-Names of Dane County, Wisconsin* (Cassidy 2009), of uncertain origin, though perhaps it is "the name of a beneficent female deity" in Sauk-Fox.

Along the shore a sign written in three languages—English, Spanish, and Hmong—warns fishermen and fisherwomen about contamination in various freshwater species (see fig. 10.1). The men fishing at Monona Terrace weren't deterred, however. They pulled flopping bluegills from the water, while on a small transistor radio Wayne Larrivee, voice of the Green Bay Packers, described a "Lambeau Leap." Monona Terrace, designed by Frank Lloyd Wright, draws tourists from the state and beyond, so I was not surprised to hear a young couple evaluating the city's skyline in voices shaped in the American South. I passed two women chatting in Russian as I walked north on Martin Luther King Jr. Boulevard toward the Capitol. A demonstration in support of regional mass transit circled counterclockwise around the brilliant granite building. Marching between a hybrid city bus and a Toyota Prius taxi, a pack of people chanted "recycle plastic, it's fantastic."

FIGURE 10.1. Signs, such as this one along the north shore of Lake Monona, are features of the linguistic landscape. The three languages on this sign—English, Spanish, and Hmong—suggest the contemporary linguistic diversity of Madison. October 2010.

When I got home that day I sketched a map of what I had seen and heard (see fig. 10.2). Although personal and informal, this map shares some basic principles with more formal maps, such as reference maps that guide us to a good supper club or thematic maps that show us the demographic complexities of our communities. A central principle of maps is that they *graphically represent spatial phenomena and relationships*; that supper club has a particular location, which is a number of miles in a certain direction from my home. But a useful road map, whether paper or digital, cannot show everything along the route; maps are *abstractions*, and this is a second principle. The level of abstraction depends on a map's scale, purpose, and, ultimately, on its maker or makers. And, as we know, people have different motives and ways of looking at the world, which maps express implicitly in addition to the spatial information that they communicate explicitly. This notion of *authorship*, as the hand-drawn map of my Sunday afternoon walkabout suggests, is a third principle characteristic of all maps.

FIGURE 10.2. Rough map of a linguistic landscape in Madison, October 2010

Linguistic maps are specialized thematic maps that chart various language features in a selected area, such as a city, state, or region (Peeters and Williams 1993). When they document aspects of people's speech and then plot the features on maps, linguists are constructing language communities based on similarities, searching for spatial patterns, and hypothesizing why those language features vary from place to place. Historical, geographic, and socioeconomic information, either added to the linguistic data or presented as separate maps, enrich the understanding of linguistic communities and language variation through time and space.

The thematic maps in this volume draw on standard techniques from the cartographer's toolkit and a variety of data sources to represent aspects of Wisconsin's linguistic landscapes, past and present (Slocum et al. 2009). Most of the maps were made using geographic data from the U.S. Census Bureau that was projected in the Albers Equal Area projection, North American Datum 1983. The challenge of representation involves identifying and organizing reputable qualitative or quantitative data and selecting the appropriate technique to map it in a way that is clear, appealing, and spatially interesting. Like a storyteller, a cartographer makes deliberate choices about what, why, and how to show something.

Choropleth maps, for example, commonly represent standardized quantitative data for enumeration units such as towns (townships) and counties. Data is categorized into classes that are shaded according to their value for each enumeration unit. In this volume, choropleth maps in Felecia Lucht's, Antje Petty's, and Catherine Stafford's chapters represent either historic or contemporary data at the county level. For these maps, data came from the U.S. Census Bureau, which has traditionally collected data regarding language use and ability, as well as complementary data on ethnicity, income, and education that can influence linguistic features, in the decennial census. In recent years, the task of collecting and reporting language data has been transferred to the American Community Survey, which is conducted on an ongoing basis.

In contrast to choropleth maps, proportional symbol maps use scaled point symbols to represent raw totals for specific locations. Maps in Thomas Purnell's and Susan Meredith Burt's chapters, for example, use proportional symbols to represent the population of African Americans and Hmong speakers in Wisconsin counties, respectively. Using proportional symbols for these maps, particularly those that incorporate additional data, offers a more interesting spatial story than shaded enumeration units showing standardized data. In Karen Washinawatok and Monica Macaulay's chapter, a proportional symbol map represents the enrollments of Indian schools in Wisconsin in 1899, historic data gathered from a report by the U.S. Department of the Interior. Related to these proportional symbol maps are dot density maps, which appear in Joseph Salmons's preface, of the four most recent U.S. census language categories. For these maps, however, dots are one size and represent one value, one hundred people.

The isogloss is a line symbol common in linguistic mapping. As its etymology suggests (Greek for "equal tongue"), the isogloss distinguishes regions of linguistic similarity, whether for words, sounds, or other aspects of speech. For noted Wisconsin linguist Frederic G. Cassidy sixty years ago, drawing isoglosses to chart the results of his statewide survey was an important part of his research method (see fig. 10.3).

When researchers determine that multiple isoglosses "bundle" in the same or adjacent locations, they often construct dialect boundaries. In this volume, for example, the isoglosses in a map in Kristin Speth's chapter situate the Iowa County community of Mineral Point near the convergence of three dialect regions—North Central, Inland North, and Upper Midlands—originally constructed by linguist William Labov and a team of researchers. The map also suggests the importance of Wisconsin talk to contemporary discussions about linguistic variation through space.

Isoglosses are normally drawn as solid lines, although in reality language is in flux and boundaries outside the controlled space of a map are most often fuzzy. This tension between the graphic authority of a map symbol and the dynamic phenomenon it represents underscores that linguistic mapping invites experimentation. One original effort has been the cartogram of the *Dictionary of American Regional English* (*DARE*), a project initiated by Cassidy over forty years ago at the University of Wisconsin–Madison that continues today. The emblematic

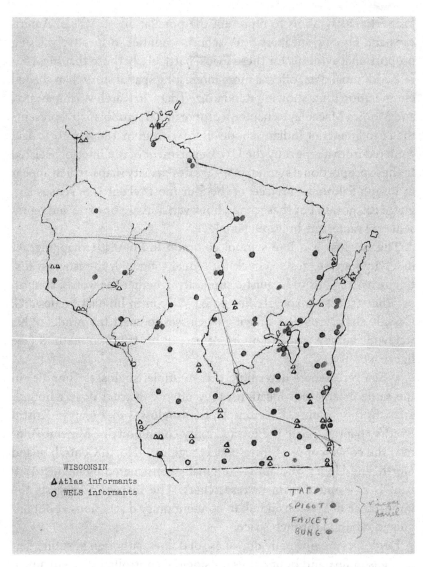

FIGURE 10.3. Map made by Frederic G. Cassidy for the Wisconsin English Language Survey showing isogloss and locations of people who used *tap, spigot, faucet,* or *bung,* ca. 1950 (Courtesy of *Dictionary of American Regional English.* A color version of the map is available online at the Wisconsin Talk website.)

DARE map, which appears in Luanne von Schneidemesser's chapter, shows regional distributions of words and phrases, collected from the *DARE* survey conducted from 1965 to 1970, relative to state population densities at that time.

As a paper map, such as those in this volume, the *DARE* cartogram implicitly reinforces a notion of language as static. Emerging interactive and animated mapping techniques, however, are potential ways to represent the reality that sounds change, new words appear, meanings morph, and the number of speakers increases or decreases through time and space. In the future, researchers will likely continue to explore ways to apply these computer technologies, as well as others such as geographic information systems, and experiment with visual variables to represent linguistic features, organize and analyze data, and generate hypotheses.

Maps invite exploration. The United States Geological Survey topographical map of Timms Hill tempts one to set out and bag the highest point in Wisconsin. The popular "Cultural Map of Wisconsin" (Woodward et al. 1996) encourages a person to hit the road, if not literally than at least in his or her imagination, in search of the names, people, and places that distinguish the state. And the maps in this volume invite a person to look out for, listen to, and ask questions about the multiple linguistic landscapes that have defined and continue to distinguish the Badger State, as I did that sunny October day in Madison.

NOTE

I would like to thank Lisa Jackson for her helpful comments about this article and Daniel P. Huffman for reviewing the maps in this volume.

Conclusion and Outlook

JOSEPH SALMONS

We have dealt throughout this short volume with a wide range of historical and contemporary languages and dialects from a variety of Wisconsin communities and from a variety of perspectives. Linguists use the present to help understand the past, and the past and present to help understand the future. These are almost always only rough guides, but they are still helpful: if we see that things consistently work a certain way now, it's not unreasonable to investigate whether they worked that way in the past. And if we've seen particular patterns repeatedly in the past, we might keep an eye out for whether current situations will unfold in similar ways. In the particular area under discussion here, the state of Wisconsin, this is likewise true.

You've seen examples of how we now understand Wisconsin's linguistic past and how it bears on our linguistic present. The many non-English-speaking people living in this state have learned English and most have abandoned other languages in favor of English. For many of them, like most Wisconsinites of German and Norwegian extraction, the passing of the ancestral language is a matter of nostalgia. In fact, the nostalgia often involves a fair bit of distance from the earlier linguistic reality. The picture reproduced here (see fig. c.1) shows what was once regarded as a stereotypical feature of Norwegian American English, the use of *y* for *j*, but even by the time of the earliest fieldwork (by Einar Haugen, for example, mentioned in the introduction), this was an uncommon feature of Norwegian American speech, even those who spoke English with a strong Norwegian accent.

We are now seeing how complex those patterns of language shift were historically, as reflected, for example, in the role of institutional support provided in many communities, and we're seeing that many current stereotypes actually don't hold, such as that these earlier immigrants learned English quickly and easily. For many others, like many people in Native American communities, the stakes are different and much higher: languages were not abandoned willingly but only under serious duress, with real damage to community structures and cultures. But there, we see resilience today with strong efforts to revitalize and support those languages. Even where English was brought by settlers, like in Mineral Point, language has changed more than we usually appreciate, and it continues to change today throughout the state. So,

FIGURE C.1. "Yon Yonson" food cart in Madison, 2011

what is the future likely to bring? Let's frame this briefly around a couple of questions to illustrate the kinds of issues we expect to be discussed and the kind of trends we expect to see.

First, will languages other than English continue to be spoken in the state? Almost certainly, they will. New people will surely continue to come to Wisconsin, and our state is already home to a steadily growing population of Pennsylvania Dutch (or "Pennsylvania German") speakers, as noted in the preface. Language revival, a critical issue in Indian communities in Wisconsin and indigenous communities worldwide, is an area where innovators are breaking new ground. Knowing the dedication and energy that tribal members are bringing to this, I'm personally optimistic that at least a number of those efforts will succeed.

Second, how will schools deal with language in the future? Educational policy, especially public education, concerning language is so driven by politics and changes in society that even casual speculation about what might happen in the future is dangerous. We obviously hope that language-related policies will be informed by the best research findings and by the lessons of history. Key among both, I would argue, is that "English only" and similar policies are directly harmful to our society. People in this country learn English—relatively few retain other languages alongside it, in fact. Indeed, the tangible advantages of being multilingual are great (as laid out plainly in chapter 9), for individuals and societies.

Third, what will happen to the distinctive kinds of English spoken in the state? It seems very safe to say that regional English will clearly continue to evolve here. It's possible, maybe likely, that it'll become more distinctive in its sounds and words and structures. If so, it would likely involve ongoing development of features already present in the state.

So, while we watch these developments unfold, however they may, and wait for a companion to this volume, our work goes on and language and the languages spoken here continue to change. Enjoy this book, and please do contact the authors and editors with your comments, ideas, and questions. We look forward to it.

References

Adams, Michael Paul. 2009. *Slang: The People's Poetry*. Oxford: Oxford University Press.

Alim, H. Samy. 2004. *You Know My Steez: An Ethnographic and Sociolinguistic Study of Styleshifting in a Black American Speech Community*. Durham, NC: Duke University Press.

Allen, Harold. 1973–76. *The Linguistic Atlas of the Upper Midwest*. 3 vols. Minneapolis: University of Minnesota Press.

Andreozzi, John. 1987. "Italian Farmers in Cumberland." In *Italian Immigrants in Rural and Small Town America: Essays from the Fourteenth Annual Conference of the American Italian Historical Association*, edited by Rudolph J. Vecoli, 110–25. New York: American Italian Historical Association.

Apps, Jerry. 2007. *In a Pickle: A Family Farm Story*. Madison, WI: Terrace Books.

"Bartosz Era Is over at 'GP.'" 1973. *Stevens Point (WI) Daily*, July 28, 6.

Baugh, John. 1988. *Black Street Speech*. Austin: University of Texas Press.

———. 1999. *Out of the Mouths of Slaves: African American Language and Educational Malpractice*. Austin: University of Texas Press.

———. 2000. *Beyond Ebonics: Linguistic Pride and Racial Prejudice*. Oxford: Oxford University Press.

Benson, Erica, Michael J. Fox, and Jared Balkman. 2011. "*The bag that Scott bought*: The Low Vowels in Northwest Wisconsin." *American Speech* 86 (3): 271–311.

Bialystok, Ellen. 2007. "Cognitive Effects of Bilingualism: How Linguistic Experience Leads to Cognitive Change." *International Journal of Bilingual Education and Bilingualism* 10 (3): 210–23.

Bialystok, Ellen, Fergus I. M. Craik, Raymond Klein, and Mythili Viswanathan. 2004. "Bilingualism, Aging, and Cognitive Control: Evidence from the Simon Task." *Psychology and Aging* 19 (2): 290–303.

Bialystok, Ellen, Fergus I. M. Craik, and A. C. Ruocco. 2006. "Dual-Modality Monitoring in a Classification Task: The Effects of Bilingualism and Ageing." *Quarterly Journal of Experimental Psychology* 59 (11): 1968–83.

Biber, Douglas, Stig Johansson, Geoffrey Leech, and Susan Conrad. 1999. *Longman Grammar of Spoken and Written English*. Harlow, UK: Longman.

Brenzinger, Matthias, Akira Yamamoto, Noriko Aikawa, Dmitri Koundiouba, Anahit Minasyan, Arienne Dwyer, Colette Grinevald, Michael Krauss, Osahito Miyaoka, Osamu Sakiyama, Rieks Smeets, and Ofelia Zepeda. 2003. "Language Vitality and Endangerment." International Expert Meeting on UNESCO Programme Safeguarding of Endangered Languages, Paris, Mar. 10–12.

Brueggemann, G. R. 1964. *By the Grace of God: The History of Trinity Evangelical Lutheran Church of Freistadt*. Vol. 2. Freistadt, WI: Trinity Evangelical Lutheran Church.

Burt, Susan Meredith. 2009. "Contact Pragmatics: Requests in Wisconsin Hmong." *Journal of the Southeast Asian Linguistics Society* 1:63–76.

———. 2010. *The Hmong Language in Wisconsin: Language Shift and Pragmatic Change*. Lewiston, NY: Edwin Mellen.

Burt, Susan Meredith, and Hua Yang. 2005. "Growing Up Shifting: Immigrant Children, Their Families, and the Schools." In *Language in the Schools: Integrating Linguistic Knowledge into K-12 Teaching*, edited by Kristin Denham and Anne Lobeck, 29–40. Mahwah, NJ: Erlbaum.

Caldwell, Alan, and Monica Macaulay. 2000. "The Current Status of the Menominee Language." *Proceedings of the 31st Conference on Algonquian Languages* 31:18–29.

Cassidy, Frederic G. 1991. "Miscousing—Wisconsin." *Names* 39 (3): 191–98.

———. 2009. *Dane County Place-Names*. 2nd ed. Madison: University of Wisconsin Press.

Cassidy, Frederic G., and Joan Houston Hall, eds. 1985–2012. *The Dictionary of American Regional English*. Cambridge, MA: Harvard University Press.

Chomsky, Noam. 2003. "The Function of Schools: Subtler and Cruder Methods of Control." In *Education as Enforcement: The Militarization and Corporatization of Schools*, edited by Kenneth Saltman and David Gabbard, 25–36. New York: Routledge.

Clyne, Michael G. 1991. *Community Languages: The Australian Experience*. Cambridge: Cambridge University Press.

Conzen, Michael P. 1997. "The European Settling and Transformation of the Upper Mississippi Valley Lead Mining Region." In *Wisconsin Land and Life*, edited by Robert C. Ostergren and Thomas R. Vale, 163–96. Madison: University of Wisconsin Press.

Copeland, Louis Albert. 1898. "The Cornish in Southwest Wisconsin." In vol. 14 of *Collections of the State Historical Society of Wisconsin*, edited by Reuben Gold Thwaites, 301–34. Madison, WI: Democrat Printing Company.

Cummins, James. 2001. "Linguistic Interdependence and the Educational Development of Bilingual Children." In *The New Immigrant and Language*, vol. 6 of *Interdisciplinary Perspectives on the New Immigration*, edited by Marcelo M. Suárez-Orozco, Carola Suárez-Orozco, and Desirée Qin-Hilliard, 72–101. New York: Routledge.

Cummins, James, and Metro Gulustan. 1974. "Some Effects of Bilingualism on Cognitive Functioning." In *Bilingualism, Biculturalism and Education*, edited by Stephen T. Carey, 129–36. Edmonton: University of Alberta Press.

Cundall, I. N. 1865. "Report." In *Annual Report of the Superintendent of Public Instruction of the State of Wisconsin for the Year Ending August 31, 1864*. Madison, WI: Atwood and Rublee.

Dillard, Joey Lee. 1973. *Black English: Its History and Usage in the United States*. New York: Random House.

Duffy, John M. 2007. *Writing from These Roots: Literacy in a Hmong-American Community*. Honolulu: University of Hawaii Press.

Equal Employment Opportunity Commission v. Target Corporation. 2007. United States Courts of Appeals, 7th Cir., case 04-3559.

Fapso, Richard J. 2001. *Norwegians in Wisconsin*. Madison: Wisconsin Historical Society Press.

Farley, Reynolds. 2000. "Racial Residential Segregation: Census: 2000 Findings." http://enceladus.isr.umich.edu/race/racestart.asp.

Fishman, Joshua A. 1991. *Reversing Language Shift*. Clevedon, UK: Multilingual Matters.

———, ed. 2001. *Can Threatened Languages Be Saved?* Buffalo, NY: Multilingual Matters.

———. 2006. "Three Hundred-Plus Years of Heritage Language Education in the United States." In *Developing Minority Language Resources: The Case of Spanish in California*, edited by Guadalupe Valdés, Joshua A. Fishman, Rebecca Chávez, and William Pérez, 12–23. Buffalo, NY: Multilingual Matters.

Fought, Carmen. 2002. "California Students' Perceptions of, You Know, Regions and Dialects?" In *Handbook of Perceptual Dialectology*, vol. 2, edited by Daniel Long and Dennis Preston, 113–34. Amsterdam: John Benjamins.

Gleason, Jean B., Rivka Y. Perlmann, and Esther B. Greif. 1984. "What's the Magic Word: Learning Language through Politeness Routines." *Discourse Processes* 7 (4): 493–502.

Goc, Michael. 1992. *Native Realm: The Polish-American Community of Portage County, 1857–1992*. Stevens Point, WI: Worzalla Publishing Company.

Goldberg, Bettina. 1995. "The German-English Academy, the National German-American Teachers' Seminary, and the Public School System in Milwaukee, Wisconsin 1851–1919." In *German Influences on Education in the United States to 1917*, edited by Henry Geitz, Jürgen Heideking, and Jurgen Herbst, 177–92. Cambridge: Cambridge University Press.

Green, Lisa. 2002. *African American English: A Linguistic Introduction*. Cambridge: Cambridge University Press.

Greene, Victor. 2009. "Dealing with Diversity: Milwaukee's Multiethnic Festivals and Urban Identity, 1840–1940." In *Perspectives on Milwaukee's Past*, edited by Margo Anderson and Victor Greene, 285–316. Urbana: University of Illinois Press.

Grosjean, François. 1998. "Studying Bilinguals: Methodological and Conceptual Issues." *Bilingualism: Language and Cognition* 1 (2): 131–49.

Hale, Frederick. 2002. *Swedes in Wisconsin*. Madison: Wisconsin Historical Society Press.

Hartley, Laura C. 1999. "A View from the West: Perceptions of U.S. Dialects by Oregon Residents." In *Handbook of Perceptual Dialectology*, vol. 1, edited by Dennis Preston, 315–31. Amsterdam: John Benjamins.

Haugen, Einar. 1953. *The Norwegian Language in America*. Philadelphia: University of Pennsylvania Press.

Hein, Jeremy. 2006. *Ethnic Origins: The Adaptation of Cambodian and Hmong Refugees in Four American Cities*. New York: American Sociological Association.

Hillmer, Paul. 2009. *A People's History of the Hmong*. St. Paul: Minnesota Historical Society Press.

Hinton, Leanne. 2001. "The Master-Apprentice Language Learning Program." In *The Green Book of Language Revitalization in Practice*, edited by Leanne Hinton and Ken Hale, 217–26. New York: Academic Press.

Holzhueter, John, interviewer. 1982. *Mineral Point Remembered*. Cassette. Madison: Wisconsin Historical Society.

Horn, Fred W. 1864. "Report." In *Message of the Governor of Wisconsin Together with an Annual Report of the Officers of the State for the Year A.D. 1863*. Madison, WI: William J. Park.

Huddleston, Rodney, and Geoffrey K. Pullum. 2005. *A Student's Introduction to English Grammar*. New York: Cambridge University Press.

Jacobi-Dittrich, Juliane. 1988. *"Deutsche" Schulen in den Vereinigten Staaten von Amerika: Historisch-vergleichende Studie zum Unterrichtswesen im Mittleren Westen (Wisconsin 1840–1900)*. Munich: Minerva Publikation.

Jewell, Jim. 1990. *Cornish in America: Linden, Wisconsin.* Linden, WI: Cornish Miner Press.

Joseph, Brian D., Carol G. Preston, and Dennis R. Preston. 2005. *Language Diversity in Michigan and Ohio: Towards Two State Linguistic Profiles.* Ann Arbor, MI: Caravan Books.

Kluge, Cora Lee, ed. 2007. *Other Witnesses: An Anthology of Literature of the German Americans, 1850–1914.* Madison, WI: Max Kade Institute.

Koltyk, Jo Ann. 1997. *New Pioneers in the Heartland: Hmong Life in Wisconsin.* Boston: Allyn and Bacon.

König, Werner. 2007. *dtv-Atlas Deutsche Sprache.* 16th ed. Munich: Deutscher Taschenbuch Verlag.

Labov, William. 1973. *Language in the Inner City: Studies in the Black English Vernacular.* Philadelphia: University of Philadelphia Press.

Labov, William, Sharon Ash, and Charles Boberg. 2006. *The Atlas of North American English: Phonetics, Phonology, and Sound Change.* Berlin: Mouton de Gruyter.

Landry, Rodrigue, and Richard Y. Bourhis. 1997. "Linguistic Landscape and Ethnolinguistic Vitality: An Empirical Study." *Journal of Language and Social Psychology* 16 (1): 23–49.

Leary, James P. 2001. *So Ole Says to Lena: Folk Humor of the Upper Midwest.* 2nd ed. Madison: University of Wisconsin Press.

Lo, Fungchatou T. 2001. *The Promised Land: Socioeconomic Reality of the Hmong People in Urban America (1976–2000).* Bristol, IN: Wyndham Hall Press.

Loew, Patty. 2001. *Indian Nations of Wisconsin: Histories of Endurance and Renewal.* Madison: Wisconsin Historical Society Press.

Lucht, Felecia. 2007. "Language Variation in a German-American Community: A Diachronic Study of the Spectrum of Language Use in Lebanon, Wisconsin." PhD diss., University of Wisconsin–Madison.

Lucht, Felecia, Benjamin Frey, and Joseph Salmons. 2011. "A Tale of Three Cities: Urban-Rural Asymmetries in Language Shift?" *Journal of Germanic Linguistics* 23 (4): 347–74.

Martin-Rhee, Michelle M., and Bialystok, Ellen. 2008. "The Development of Two Types of Inhibitory Control in Monolingual and Bilingual Children." *Bilingualism: Language and Cognition* 11 (1): 81–93.

McHugh, Kevin. 1987. "Black Migration Reversal in the United States." *Geographical Review* 77 (2): 171–82.

Meinig, Donald W., ed. 1979. *The Interpretation of Ordinary Landscapes: Geographical Essays.* New York: Oxford University Press.

Merrill, Peter C. 2000. *German-American Urban Culture: Writers and Theaters in Early Milwaukee.* Madison, WI: Max Kade Institute.

Millar, Robert McColl. 2008. "The Origins and Development of Shetland Dialect in Light of Dialect Contact Theories." *English World-Wide* 29 (3): 237–67.

Mufwene, Salikoko. 2001. "What Is African American English?" In *Sociocultural and Historical Contexts of African American English*, edited by Sonja Lanehart, 21–52. Amsterdam: John Benjamins.

Nash, Manning. 1989. *The Cauldron of Ethnicity in the Modern World*. Chicago: University of Chicago Press.

Neal, Robert. 1955. *Robert Neal*. Cassette. Madison: Wisconsin Historical Society.

Nesbit, Robert C. 1989. *Wisconsin: A History*. 2nd ed. Madison: University of Wisconsin Press.

Nollendorfs, Cora Lee. 1988. "The First World War and the Survival of German Studies: With a Tribute to Alexander R. Hohlfeld." In *Teaching German in America*, edited by David P. Benseler, Walter F. W. Lohnes, and Valters Nollendorfs, 176–95. Madison: University of Wisconsin Press.

Oehlerts, Donald E. 1958. *Guide to Wisconsin Newspapers, 1833–1957*. Madison: State Historical Society of Wisconsin.

Ostergren, Robert C. 1997. "The Euro-American Settlement of Wisconsin, 1830–1920." In *Wisconsin Land and Life*, edited by Robert C. Ostergren and Thomas R. Vale, 137–62. Madison: University of Wisconsin Press.

Padgett, Deborah. 1989. *Settlers and Sojourners: A Study of Serbian Adaptation in Milwaukee, Wisconsin*. New York: AMS Press.

Parker, Frank, and Kathryn Riley. 2010. *Linguistics for Non-Linguists: A Primer with Exercises*. Allyn and Bacon.

Paulson, Arthur C., and Kenneth O. Bjork. 1938. "A School and Language Controversy in 1858: A Documentary Study." In *Publications of the Norwegian American Historical Association*. Northfield, MN: Norwegian American Historical Society.

Peeters, Yvo J. D., and Colin H. Williams, eds. 1992. *The Cartographic Representation of Linguistic Data. Discussion Papers in Geolinguistics*, Nos. 19–21. Staffordshire, UK: Staffordshire University.

Pfeifer, Mark E. 2006. "Southeast Asian American Data 2006 American Community Survey." http://www.hmongstudies.org/SEA2006ACS.html.

Pomeroy, F. C. 1867. "Report." In *Annual Report of the Superintendent of Public Instruction of the State of Wisconsin for the Year Ending August 31, 1867*. Madison, WI: Atwood and Rublee.

———. 1869. "Report." In *Annual Report of the Superintendent of Public Instruction of the State of Wisconsin for the Year Ending August 31, 1869*. Madison, WI: Atwood and Rublee.

Potowski, Kim, and Richard Cameron, eds. 2007. *Spanish in Contact: Policy, Social and Linguistic Inquiries*. Amsterdam: John Benjamins.

Preston, Dennis. 1998. "They Speak Really Bad English Down South and in New York City." In *Language Myths*, edited by Laurie Bauer and Peter Trudgill, 139–49. London: Penguin.

Purnell, Thomas. 2009. "Convergence and Contact in Milwaukee: Evidence from Select African American and White Vowel Space Features." *Journal of Language and Social Psychology* 28 (4): 408–27.

Purnell, Thomas, William Idsardi, and John Baugh. 1999. "Perceptual and Phonetic Experiments on American English Dialect Identification." *Journal of Language and Social Psychology* 18 (1): 10–30.

Rannells, Jean Saul, interviewer. 1985. *Rural Women's Oral History Project*. Cassette. Madison: Wisconsin Historical Society.

Ranney, Joseph. 1995. "Looking Further Than the Skin: A History of Wisconsin Civil Rights Law." *Wisconsin Lawyer* 68, no. 7 (July): 20–23, 52–53.

Ratliff, Martha. 1997. "Hmong-Mien Demonstratives and Pattern Persistence." *Mon-Khmer Studies* 27:317–28.

———. 2010. *Hmong-Mien Language History*. Canberra: Pacific Linguistics.

Rechcigl, Miloslav, Jr. 2005. *Czechs and Slovaks in America*. Boulder, CO: East European Monographs.

Remlinger, Kathryn, Luanne von Schneidemesser, and Joseph Salmons. 2009. "Revised Perceptions: Changing Dialect Perceptions in Wisconsin and Michigan's Upper Peninsula." *American Speech* 84 (2): 177–91.

Rickford, John. 1999. *African American Vernacular English: Features, Evolution, Educational Implications*. Oxford, UK: Blackwell.

Salmons, Joseph. 2002. "The Shift from German to English, World War I and the German-language Press in Wisconsin." In *Menschen zwischen zwei Welten: Auswanderung, Ansiedlung, Akkulturation*, edited by Walter G. Rödel and Helmut Schmahl, 178–93. Trier: Wissenschaftlicher Verlag Trier.

Scharinger, Mathias, Philip Monahan, and William Idsardi. 2011. "You had me at 'Hello': Rapid Extraction of Dialect Information from Spoken Words." *Neuroimage* 56 (4): 2329–38.

Schereck, William J., interviewer. 1955. *Ethnic History of Wisconsin*. Cassette. Madison, WI: Wisconsin Historical Society.

Simpson, Mrs. Jefferson. 1953. *Mrs. Jefferson Simpson*. Cassette. Madison, WI: Wisconsin Historical Society.

Slocum, Terry A., Robert B. McMaster, Fritz C. Kessler, and Hugh H. Howard. 2009. *Thematic Cartography and Geovisualization*. 3rd ed. Upper Saddle River, NJ: Pearson Prentice Hall.

Smith, Alice E. 1973. *From Exploration to Statehood*. Vol. 1 of *The History of Wisconsin*. Madison: State Historical Society of Wisconsin.

Smith, Andrea. 2007. "Soul Wound: The Legacy of Native American Schools." *Amnesty International Magazine*, Mar. 26. http://www.amnestyusa.org/node/87342.

Smith, Tovia. 2001. "Linguistic Profiling." *Morning Edition*, NPR, Sep. 5. http://www.npr.org/templates/story/story.php?storyId=1128513.

Smitherman, Geneva. 1977. *Talkin and Testifyin: The Language of Black America.* Detroit, MI: Wayne State University Press.

———. 1994. *Black Talk: Words and Phrases from the Hood to the Amen Corner.* Detroit, MI: Wayne State University Press.

Strohschänk, Johannes, and William G. Thiel. 2005. *The Wisconsin Office of Emigration, 1852–1855, and Its Impact on German Immigration to the State.* Madison, WI: Max Kade Institute.

———. 2006. "The Wisconsin Commissioner of Emigration 1852–1855: An Experiment in Social and Economic Engineering and Its Impact on German Immigration to Wisconsin." In *Wisconsin German Land and Life*, edited by Heike Bungert, Cora Lee Kluge, and Robert C. Ostergren, 93–121. Madison, WI: Max Kade Institute.

Tomlinson, Carol. 1999. *The Differentiated Classroom: Responding to the Needs of All Learners.* Alexandria, VA: Association for Supervision and Curriculum Development.

———. 2003. *Fulfilling the Promise of the Differentiated Classroom: Strategies and Tools for Responsive Teaching.* Alexandria, VA: Association for Supervision and Curriculum Development.

Toth, Carolyn. 1990. *German-English Bilingual Schools in America.* New York: Peter Lang.

Trotter, Joe William, Jr. 1985. *Black Milwaukee: The Making of an Industrial Proletariat, 1915–1945.* Urbana: University of Illinois Press.

Trudgill, Peter. 2004. *New-Dialect Formation: The Inevitability of Colonial Englishes.* Edinburgh: Edinburgh University Press.

Tyrer, Howard. 1966. *Howard Tyrer.* Cassette. Madison, WI: Wisconsin Historical Society.

Upton, Clive, and J. D. A. Widdowson. 1996. *An Atlas of English Dialects.* Oxford: Oxford University Press.

U.S. Census Bureau. 1890. "Report on Population of the United States 1890, Part I, Foreign Born Population, Table 32." http://www2.census.gov/prod2/decennial/documents/1890a_v1-16.pdf.

———. 2000. "Table DP-1. Profile of General Demographic Characteristics, Geographic Area: Wisconsin." http://www.census.gov/census2000/states/wi.html.

———. 2006. "United States—Selected Population Profile in the United States (Hmong)." http://www.hmongstudies.org/SEA2006ACS.html.

————. 2006–10. "American Community Survey." http://www.census.gov/acs.

Valdés, Guadalupe. 2005. "Bilingualism, Heritage Language Learners, and SLA Research: Opportunities Lost or Seized?" *Modern Language Journal* 89 (3): 410–26.

Veltman, Calvin. 1983. *Language Shift in the United States.* Berlin: Walter de Gruyter.

Viertes Lesebuch für die deutschen katholischen Schulen in den Vereinigten Staaten von Nord-Amerika. 1874. New York: Verlag von Benziger Brothers.

Vogel, Virgil J. 1991. *Indian Names on Wisconsin's Map.* Madison: University of Wisconsin Press.

Wilkerson, Miranda E., and Joseph Salmons. 2008. "'Good Old Immigrants of Yesteryear' Who Didn't Learn English: Germans in Wisconsin." *American Speech* 83 (3): 259–83.

Williams, Robert L. 1975. *Ebonics: The True Language of Black Folks.* St. Louis, MO: Institute of Black Studies.

Wisconsin Cartographers' Guild. 1998. *Wisconsin's Past and Present: A Historical Atlas.* Madison: University of Wisconsin Press.

Wisconsin Staats-Einwanderungs-Behörde. 1853. *Handbuch zum Nutzen und Besten der Einwanderer.* Madison, WI: Staats-Einwanderungs-Behörde.

Wisconsin State Legislature. 1848. *An Act in Relation to Public Schools.* In *Laws of Wisconsin,* 226–47. Madison, WI: Rhenodyne Bird.

————. 1889. *Laws of Wisconsin.* Vol. 1. Madison, WI: Democrat Printing Company.

Wolfram, Walt. 1969. *A Sociolinguistic Description of Detroit Negro Speech.* Washington, DC: Center for Applied Linguistics.

Wolfram, Walt, and Natalie Schilling-Estes. 2006. *American English.* Oxford, UK: Blackwell.

Woodward, David, Robert Ostergren, Onno Brouwer, Steven Hoelscher, and Joshua Hane. 1996. *Cultural Map of Wisconsin: A Cartographic Portrait of the State.* Madison: University of Wisconsin Press.

Wurm, Stephen. 1991. "Language Death and Disappearance: Causes and Circumstances." In *Endangered Languages,* edited by Robert H. Robins and Eugenius M. Uhlenbeck, 1–18. Oxford, UK: Berg.

Zaniewski, Kazimierz J., and Carol J. Rosen. 1998. *The Atlas of Ethnic Diversity in Wisconsin.* Madison: University of Wisconsin Press.

Contributors

SUSAN MEREDITH BURT is a professor of linguistics in the Department of English at Illinois State University and the author of *The Hmong Language in Wisconsin*. She lives in Normal, Illinois, but hopes someday to return to Wisconsin for projects linguistic, folkloric, and/or terpsichorean.

MARK LIVENGOOD, folklorist and cartographer, is Grant Program Manager for the Wisconsin Humanities Council. He speaks the Inland North dialect of northwest Ohio, where he grew up.

FELECIA LUCHT is an assistant professor in the Department of Classical and Modern Languages, Literatures and Cultures at Wayne State University. She earned a PhD in Germanic linguistics from the University of Wisconsin–Madison and specializes in German American studies and language contact. Her research interests include language maintenance and shift, language change, code switching, pedagogy, and second language acquisition.

MONICA MACAULAY is a professor of linguistics at the University of Wisconsin–Madison and specializes in the morphology of American Indian languages. She has worked on Chalcatongo Mixtec, Ojitlán Chinantec, Karuk, Menominee, and Potawatomi. She has produced two dictionaries of Menominee and is part of a group that is working on a dictionary of Potawatomi. She is also one of the review editors for the LINGUIST List and is the author of *Surviving Linguistics: A Guide for Graduate Students*.

ANTJE PETTY is the assistant director at the Max Kade Institute for German-American Studies at the University of Wisconsin–Madison, where she researches the stories of German-speaking immigrants and their descendants in a global, multicultural, and interdisciplinary context and shares the institute's resources with communities throughout the state.

THOMAS PURNELL is an associate professor in the Department of English at the University of Wisconsin–Madison. His research and teaching examine the interface between phonetics and phonology with a focus on regional pronunciation. In particular, he is interested in the intersection of ethnically affiliated social groups and the sound systems of language.

ERIC RAIMY is an associate professor of English language and linguistics in the Department of English at the University of Wisconsin–Madison. He researches phonology from a cognitive science point of view. He has recently coedited two volumes with Charles Cairns, *Contemporary Views on Architecture and Representations in Phonology* and *Handbook of the Syllable*, that came out of their organization of the CUNY Phonology Forum Conferences. He is an active participant in the Wisconsin Englishes Project.

JOSEPH SALMONS serves as the Lester W. J. "Smoky" Seifert Professor of Germanic Linguistics at the University of Wisconsin–Madison. His research, teaching, and outreach work all focus on speech sounds and language change, drawing data particularly from Germanic languages, including Wisconsin English past and present. He is the author of *A History of German: What the Past Reveals about Today's Language* and the executive editor of *Diachronica: International Journal for Historical Linguistics*.

LUANNE VON SCHNEIDEMESSER, senior editor of the *Dictionary of American Regional English* (*DARE*) and Distinguished Scientist at the University of Wisconsin–Madison, holds a PhD in German linguistics. Her publication topics include *DARE* and regional American English, of course, as well as *pop* and *soda*, terms used in children's games, the dialect vocabulary of the Upper Midwest and Kansas, German influences on English, use of digital resources, and outreach. She has served on the ACLS Board of Directors, is a fellow of the Dictionary Society of North America, and is currently president of the American Dialect Society. She is part of the Wisconsin Englishes Project, headquartered at UW–Madison.

PEYTON SMITH is a lifelong and proud Wisconsinite and an emeritus assistant vice chancellor at the University of Wisconsin–Madison. Throughout his career he worked to advance the Wisconsin Idea by helping to extend the resources and knowledge of the university to the people of the state and nation.

KRISTIN SPETH is currently writing her doctoral dissertation in the Department of German at the University of Wisconsin–Madison. Her primary focus is on the historical Germanic languages. Her other recent research includes an investigation of the "founder effect" in Mineral Point and the maintenance of heritage Norwegian in parts of Minnesota and Wisconsin.

CATHERINE STAFFORD is an associate professor of Spanish linguistics and second language acquisition in the Department of Spanish and Portuguese at the University of Wisconsin–Madison. Her research interests include the effects of age, memory, and instructional explicitness on second language acquisition and bilingual cognition during language learning and use. She has authored and coauthored papers on these topics that have been published or are forthcoming in *Applied Linguistics, Language Teaching Research, Language Learning, International Journal of Bilingual Education and Bilingualism,* and *International Journal of Multilingualism.*

KAREN WASHINAWATOK earned her master's degree from the College of Education at the University of Arizona, where she worked with the American Indian Language Development Institute. She has served on the Menominee Language and Culture Commission since 1997, the last four years serving as the director. She is a member of the Menominee Indian School Board in addition to actively collaborating with various linguistic and cultural programs locally, regionally, and nationally.

Index